T0392664

Indirect Translation

In an effort to counter the marginalization of indirect translation in systematic research, this book establishes innovative theoretical and methodological grounds and mitigates terminological instability in the field.

In so doing, it unsettles the binary paradigms still predominant in translation research, such as original versus translation and source versus target culture/language/text. The contributors focus on the indirect translation of literature and cover a variety of European and Asian cultures and languages, such as Assamese, Bengali, Catalan, Chinese, Hindi, Japanese, Kannada, Malayalam, Marathi, Oriya, Russian, Spanish, Swedish, Tamil and Urdu.

This book will be of interest to all researchers studying intercultural relations, the probabilistic genealogies of texts, the circulation of texts and ideas among dominant and dominated cultures and groups, and the implications of English as a main pivot language in today's world.

This book was originally published as a special issue of *Translation Studies*.

Alexandra Assis Rosa is an Assistant Professor in the School of Arts and Humanities at the University of Lisbon, and a researcher in Translation Studies at the University of Lisbon Centre for English Studies CEAUL/ULICES, Portugal. She has published on translation of dialect, forms of address, the communicative structure of translated narrative, censorship, retranslation and indirect translation.

Hanna Pięta is a Postdoctoral Researcher at the University of Lisbon Centre for English Studies CEAUL/ULICES, Portugal. With interests in indirect translation, centre – periphery relations, bibliometrics, translation history and translator training, she has published in the fields of Translation Studies and Iberian – Slavonic Studies.

Rita Bueno Maia is an Assistant Professor at Universidade Católica Portuguesa, Portugal, and a researcher at the Research Centre for Communication and Culture, Lisbon, Portugal. With interests in indirect translation, pseudotranslation, translator training, exile, Iberian relations and book history, she has published in the fields of Translation Studies and Iberian Studies.

Indirect Translation

Theoretical, Methodological and
Terminological Issues

Edited by
**Alexandra Assis Rosa, Hanna Pięta and
Rita Bueno Maia**

LONDON AND NEW YORK

First published 2019
by Routledge
2 Park Square, Milton Park, Abingdon, Oxon, OX14 4RN

and by Routledge
52 Vanderbilt Avenue, New York, NY 10017

Routledge is an imprint of the Taylor & Francis Group, an informa business

© 2019 Taylor & Francis

British Library Cataloguing-in-Publication Data
A catalogue record for this book is available from the British Library

ISBN13: 978-0-367-19946-3

Typeset in Minion Pro
by codeMantra

Publisher's Note
The publisher accepts responsibility for any inconsistencies that may have arisen during the conversion of this book from journal articles to book chapters, namely the inclusion of journal terminology.

Disclaimer
Every effort has been made to contact copyright holders for their permission to reprint material in this book. The publishers would be grateful to hear from any copyright holder who is not here acknowledged and will undertake to rectify any errors or omissions in future editions of this book.

Contents

Citation Information

The chapters in this book were originally published in the *Translation Studies* journal, volume 10, issue 2 (May 2017). When citing this material, please use the original page numbering for each article, as follows:

Chapter 1
Introduction: Theoretical, methodological and terminological issues regarding indirect translation: An overview
Alexandra Assis Rosa, Hanna Pięta and Rita Bueno Maia
Translation Studies, volume 10, issue 2 (May 2017) pp. 113–132

Chapter 2
Indirectness in literary translation: Methodological possibilities
Maialen Marin-Lacarta
Translation Studies, volume 10, issue 2 (May 2017) pp. 133–149

Chapter 3
Arguing for indirect translations in twenty-first-century Scandinavia
Cecilia Alvstad
Translation Studies, volume 10, issue 2 (May 2017) pp. 150–165

Chapter 4
Institutionalized intermediates: Conceptualizing Soviet practices of indirect literary translation
Susanna Witt
Translation Studies, volume 10, issue 2 (May 2017) pp. 166–182

Chapter 5
Indirect translation and discursive identity: Proposing the concatenation effect hypothesis
James Hadley
Translation Studies, volume 10, issue 2 (May 2017) pp. 183–197

Chapter 6

Theoretical, methodological and terminological issues in researching indirect translation:
A critical annotated bibliography
Hanna Pięta
Translation Studies, volume 10, issue 2 (May 2017) pp. 198–216

For any permission-related enquiries please visit:
http://www.tandfonline.com/page/help/permissions

Notes on Contributors

Cecilia Alvstad is a Professor in the Department of Swedish Language and Multilingualism at Stockholm University, Sweden. She specializes in translation studies and has also worked on travel writing, in particular Nordic writing about Latin America.

Alexandra Assis Rosa is an Assistant Professor in the School of Arts and Humanities at the University of Lisbon, Portugal, and a researcher in Translation Studies at the University of Lisbon Centre for English Studies CEAUL/ULICES, Portugal. She has published on translation of dialect, forms of address, the communicative structure of translated narrative, censorship, retranslation and indirect translation.

Rita Bueno Maia is an Assistant Professor at Universidade Católica Portuguesa, Portugal, and a researcher at the Research Centre for Communication and Culture, Lisbon, Portugal. With interests in indirect translation, pseudotranslation, translator training, exile, Iberian relations and book history, she has published in the fields of Translation Studies and Iberian Studies.

James Hadley is Ussher Assistant Professor in Literary Translation at the Trinity Centre for Literary Translation and the School of Languages, Literatures, and Cultural Studies at Trinity College Dublin, Ireland. His research is representative of his wide-ranging interests, many of which centre on historical cases of translation in under-researched cultural contexts, particularly in East Asia.

Maialen Marin-Lacarta is an Assistant Professor at the Centre for Translation at Hong Kong Baptist University, Kowloon Tong. Among other authors, she has translated Shen Congwen in Spanish and Mo Yan in Basque. Her research areas include literary translation, Chinese literature, literary reception, translation history and digital publishing.

Hanna Pięta is a Postdoctoral Researcher at the University of Lisbon Centre for English Studies CEAUL/ULICES, Portugal. With interests in indirect translation, centre–periphery relations, bibliometrics, translation history and translator training, she has published in the fields of Translation Studies and Iberian–Slavonic Studies.

Susanna Witt is a Senior Lecturer in Russian Literature at Stockholm University, Sweden, and an affiliated researcher at the Uppsala Centre for Russian and Eurasian Studies at Uppsala University, Sweden. A specialist in Boris Pasternak's poetry and prose, she has also published widely on topics related to Russian translation history of the Soviet period.

Foreword

Alexandra Assis Rosa, Hanna Pięta and Rita Bueno Maia

Indirect translation understood as a translation of a translation is a long-standing practice applied to several text types which has so far not been subject to systematic research. As a consequence, terminology for this phenomenon is marked by considerable instability, the conceptual framework so far produced and published in scattered channels requires further reflection and sophistication; the methodologies for efficiently and effectively researching indirect translation are still partial. This volume has been organized with the purpose of contributing to mitigate terminological instability, and offer innovative theoretical and methodological proposals based on a thorough consideration of the state of the art.

The initial research article by **Assis Rosa, Pięta and Bueno Maia** offers an overview of the field. It starts by considering main claims and assumptions on indirect translation as well as main motivations for indirect translation; it intends to contribute to the standardization of the metalanguage used to research this phenomenon (regarding both the process and end text, as well as intervening languages and texts) by suggesting more transparent designations for the various subtypes of indirect translation phenomena. In order to better describe, understand and explain indirect translation, it distinguishes several types of indirectness based on specific criteria (such as the number of texts, intervening languages, and the degree, presentation and status of indirectness) to propose an innovative classification and an open set of relevant variables. Specific methodological issues are also addressed for identifying indirect translation based on textual and paratextual information, ascertaining the nature and degree of indirectness, and performing a comparative macro- and micro-textual analysis.

For a panoramic and balanced overview on this topic, each article in this volume was intended to bring expertise in a different linguaculture, stressing main concepts, findings and methods, as well as highlighting difficulties encountered and benefits gained from conducting a particular line of research.

Lacarta's article provides very useful guidelines for researchers dealing with indirect translation. The author begins by listing bibliographic sources relevant to the study of indirect translations and explaining their pros and cons. She then guides the researcher, first, through the analysis of the paratext and, afterwards, through the textual comparison between the ultimate target text and possible mediating texts. Finally, she provides convincing arguments in favour of a sociological approach to the study of indirectness. All in all, Marin Lacarta offers an overview of the research questions posed by recent works on indirect translation and indicates intriguing possibilities for future research, such as the importation of new research methods from neighbouring disciplines.

Alvstad presents a reflection on collaborative indirect translation, based on the case study of a contemporary Swedish series of eleven books translated indirectly into Swedish from

Assamese, Bengali, Hindi, Kannada, Malayalam, Marathi, Oriya, Tamil or Urdu. Against a backdrop of generalized negative evaluation of indirect translation which also influences decision makers and financing institutions, the paper analyses the arguments in favour of indirect translation put forth in the *Indiska biblioteket* (Indian library) series.

Witt draws on extensive archival sources to present an overview of the main issues raised by the extensive practice of indirect translation by means of the use of interlinear interme- diates in the Soviet Union. This practice was part of a large-scale translation project for the purpose of creating a Soviet literature. On the one hand, such practices thrived, as they were institutionalized since the early 1930s, both by means of special administrative treatment within the literary system and by means of educational efforts. On the other hand, they were argued and criticized, thus producing a very prolific corpus for research on indirect transla- tion. More importantly, this case study on the use of the so-called *podstrochniki* proves the advantages of considering a flexible definition of indirect translation, also covering cases where the mediating text is produced in the ultimate target language, for the only purpose of producing an ultimate target text.

Hadley suggests the consideration of a "concatenation effect hypothesis" according to which indirect translations are particularly prone to omit or replace cultural specificities belonging to the source language, culture and text. The author builds a case by resorting to the categories of the discursive identity spectrum proposed by Robyns and by testing this hypothesis by presenting selected information collected from published case studies on in- direct translations from a broad range of different languages and cultures.

This volume ends with an extensive (though selective) critical and annotated bibliography by **Pięta**, which contributes to presenting this volume as a desirable stepping stone for fur- ther research on the phenomenon of indirect translation.

Acknowledgements

This volume is based on a special issue of *Translation Studies* 10:2 (2017), which developed from a conference on "Voice in Indirect Translation" held at the University of Lisbon (JET1 2013), as well as from a panel presented at the 2013 Congress of the European Society for Translation Studies.

The work of Hanna Pięta and Rita Bueno Maia was supported by the Fundação para a Ciência e a Tecnologia under Grants SFRH/BPD/100800/2014 and SFRH/BPD/97092/2013, respectively.

The editors are very grateful to Giuliano d'Amico, Brian Baer, Michael Boyden, Dirk Delabastita, Cay Dollerup, João Ferreira Duarte, Javier Franco, Yves Gambier, Sehnaz Tahir Gürçaglar, Krisztina Karoly, Nike Pokorn, Clem Robyns, Esther Torres Simón, Christine Zurbach for their helpful and fruitful feedback, as well as to the general editors of the journal *Translation Studies* for their constructive assistance throughout the editing process of the special issue (10:2, 2017) on which this volume is based.

Theoretical, methodological and terminological issues regarding indirect translation: An overview

Alexandra Assis Rosa ⓘ, Hanna Pięta ⓘ and Rita Bueno Maia ⓘ

The practice of indirect translation (ITr), here understood as a translation of a translation (see Gambier 1994, 413; 2003, 57), has a long-standing history (e.g. the Bible, *I Ching*, Shakespeare translation or the activity of the so-called Toledo School), widespread use in various areas of today's society (e.g. audiovisual, computer-assisted and literary translation, localization) and, arguably, a promising future (e.g. due to globalization and the increasingly high number of working languages in international organizations, which entails editing documents via the linguae francae). Despite all this, ITr has traditionally attracted only marginal attention from translation scholars and only in recent years has it become a more popular concept in translation studies (TS) research. This growing popularity is evident from the noticeable surge in the number of scientific publications (see Pięta 2017, in this special issue) and academic events (e.g. those held in Barcelona, Germersheim and Lisbon in 2013), as well as the founding in 2016 of an international network of researchers working on ITr (IndirecTrans, www.indirectrans.com). Such developments have made a significant contribution by, for example, challenging the conventional binarism in the study of translation or offering insights into the historiography of intercultural relationships and the complex role of intermediary centres in the cross-cultural transfer between peripheries. However, ITr research remains very fragmented and this concept is thus still largely undertheorized, and its position within TS still marginal. Research has not kept pace with the rapidly evolving practice.

In an effort to overcome this fragmentation, launch this area of research from a scientific basis and accelerate the production of (a common core of) knowledge, this special issue will shed light on the state of the art of research on ITr, expand/challenge current understanding of this practice and reflect on future research avenues. Our focus is on conceptual, terminological and methodological issues.

Claims, assumptions and motivations

Before addressing the main terminological, theoretical and methodological issues, it may be useful to identify claims, assumptions and motivations regarding indirect translation. It is said to be a common practice. Given an apparently still predominant demand for closeness to the source text (ST), ITr tends to be negatively evaluated because it arguably increases the distance to the ultimate ST and, therefore, is often hidden or camouflaged.

If translation is deemed bad, because derivative, ITr is worse. It is said to be more frequent in the reception of (geographically, culturally and linguistically) distant literary
systems (but see e.g. Maia 2010, for counter examples), decreasing as relations become
closer. It is also claimed that ITr is followed by direct translation, whenever retranslation
occurs (but ample proof against this also abounds). Historically, ITr appears to decrease
when adequacy or source-orientedness prevails, but increase when acceptability or
target-orientedness prevails (Boulogne 2009; Ringmar 2007; Toury 2012). Due to globalization, ITr apparently increases, given that within an international network of power
relations, intercultural text transfer is often mediated by dominant systems. As a consequence, ITr tends to be done from one peripheral language into another via a central or
hypercentral language within the world system or the regional system of translation
(Heilbron 2010).

As for motivations, it apparently occurs due to a lack of translators or of linguistic competence in the ultimate SL, or due to difficulty obtaining the original text or translating
from a geographically and/or structurally distant language. The higher price of translating
from a distant language, as well as power relations between languages, cultures and agents
within the world translation system are also mentioned as possible causes for ITr (for
additional reasons, see e.g. Washbourne 2013).

Terminological issues

If we choose to tread an onomasiological path, ITr, defined as translation of a translation
(see Gambier 1994, 413), has developed a metalanguage often described as "messy" (Pym
2011, 80). Many publications in the field regret this terminological instability (often perceived as a symptom of undertheorization), but the overwhelming majority do not justify
their terminological choices. Metalinguistic surveys are even less common (but see
Ringmar 2007, 2–3; Pięta 2012, 13; Schultze 2014), as are explicit attempts to promote
a certain degree of terminological standardization (but see Pym 2011, 80).

Taking a different viewpoint, and informed by a conviction that terminological and
semantic diversity does not necessarily mean metalinguistic confusion, this section aims
to help put some order into the metalanguage of ITr research and increase awareness
of terminological and semantic differences. Accordingly, it will systematize some of the
most salient terminological and semantic discrepancies, pinpoint noticeable terminological and semantic patterns, consider some causes and effects of metalinguistic instability,
and make recommendations as to those needing urgent solution related to the concept
of ITr. The underlying rationale is that ITr research – and TS in general – should strive
for a discourse that (a) is unambiguous and harmonized (but not completely uniform);
(b) optimizes (rather than unnecessarily multiplies) the already rich repertoire of terms
and their meanings; and (c) cultivates "an awareness of differences in usage and where
terms are clearly defined within the language and the school of thought for which they
apply" (Snell-Hornby 2007, 322).

This section focuses on the metalanguage used by scholars rather than practitioners (for
the simple reason that there is not enough data available on the latter, but see e.g. Brodie
[2013]) and in English (mainly because in most other languages ITr terminology appears
to be largely underdeveloped).[1]

Terminological discrepancies

When acknowledging the metalinguistic diversity, studies tend to refer to discrepancies between terms denoting the ITr *process* and/or its *end text*. Since an exhaustive listing would be impossible here, Table 1 presents only a selection of terms.

However, the discrepancies are also evident in terms used for the language of the ultimate TT, as well as for other intervening texts and their corresponding languages. Illustrative snapshots of this divergent terminology are offered in Tables 2–4.

As shown in Tables 1–4, while different terms are often used with the same or analogous meaning, the same terms are also often used with different meanings. Such terminological and conceptual instability, evidenced by cases of synonymy and polysemy, can be seen in TS in general (Van Vaerenbergh 2007), so it seems unrealistic to expect ITr research to be an exception. However, in line with the rationale laid down we propose that, when analysing the chain of texts and languages in the process considered here, it may be more beneficial to use the following designations: *the ultimate ST/SL > mediating text/language > ultimate TT/TL*. It should be stressed that these terms do not imply that further action or research may not change their status.

Additionally, when referring to the process and/or its ultimate TT, the use of "indirect translation" may also be more beneficial because:

- unlike, for example, "pivot" or "relay" translation, which describe the action of the translator producing the mediating text, it describes the much more significant (Pym 2011, 80) action of the translator working from the mediating text;
- unlike, for example, "relay" or "retranslation", it has a straightforward antonym (i.e. direct translation);
- it seems a convenient umbrella term to encompass various hyponyms (e.g. "compilative", "second-hand translation"; see "Towards a Classification" below).

Table 1. Selected terms for the process and/or the end text (in alphabetic order; bolding designates terms appearing in more than one table).

Term	Example of a source	Designation of:
compilative translation	Popovič (1976)	process and end text
double translation	Edström (1991, 11)	process and end text
eclectic translation	Ringmar (2007, 3)	process and end text
end target text	Ringmar (2012, 141)	end text
final translation	Xu (1998, 11)	end text
indirect translation	Špirk (2014, 137)	process and end text
intermediate translation	Toury (1988, 139)	process and end text
mediated translation	Linder (2014, 58)	process and end text
pivot translation	Vermeulen (2012)	process
receptor text	Edström (1991, 4)	end text
relay (translation)	Dollerup (2000, 19)	process
relayed translation	Dollerup (2014, 20)	end text
retranslation (re-translation)	Bauer (1999, 20)	process
second-hand translation	Popovič (1976, 19)	process
secondary, tertiary etc. translation	Ringmar (2015, 169)	end text
T2	Washbourne (2013, 607)	end text
target text	Špirk (2014, 137)	end text
ultimate target text	Pięta (2012, 313)	end text

Table 2. Selected terms for the end text's language (in alphabetic order; bolding designates terms appearing in more than one table).

Term	Source
language C	Landers (2001, 130)
target language	Toury (1988, 139)
third language	St André (2009, 230)
ultimate target language	Pięta (2012, 313)

Regarding terminological preferences, it must be acknowledged that some choices may have been somewhat influenced by the researchers' national/linguistic and school/branch affiliations. For example, the choice of "indirect translation" may have been modelled on *tradução indirecta*, the corresponding term in Portuguese, which has been the main source or target language in our research. Additionally, since our research has been strongly anchored in descriptive approaches to translation, it must be acknowledged that that the labelling "indirect translation" and "ultimate SL" is related to the impact of the use of such terms by Gideon Toury (1995), a founding father of DTS.

Table 3. Selected terms for the intervening text (in alphabetic order; bolding designates terms appearing in more than one table).

Term	Source
first-hand translation	Toury (1995, 129)
indirect translation	Washbourne (2013, 608)
intermediate translation (text/version)	Shuttleworth and Cowie (1997, 76)
intermediary translation (text/version)	Dollerup (2000, 19)
mediating text (translation/version)	Pięta (2012, 313)
original (text)	Dollerup (2000, 18)
original source text	Edström (1991, 4)
pivot (translation)	Grigaravičiūte and Gottlieb (1999, 46)
primary source (text/translation/version)	Kittel (1991)
relay translation	Washbourne (2013)
source text	Landers (2001)
target text	Toury (1995)
ultimate original	Toury (1995, 129)
ultimate source text	Pięta (2012, 313)

Table 4. Selected terms for the intervening languages (in alphabetic order; bolding designates terms appearing in more than one table).

Term	Source
clearing house (language)	St André (2010, 86)
gateway language	Chengzhou (2001, 197)
intermediary language	Dollerup (2014, 30)
language A, B	Landers (2001, 130)
mediating language	Pięta (2012, 313)
mediator language	Edström (1991, 3)
middle language	Hyung-jin (2008, 77)
original source language	Landers (2001, 130)
pivot language	Grigaravičiūte and Gottlieb (1999, 46)
relay language	Hyung-jin (2008, 77)
second, **third language**, etc.	Hyung-jin (2008, 77)
source language	Chengzhou (2001, 197)
target language	Dollerup (2000, 18)
transmitter language	Edström (1991, 4)
ultimate source language	Toury (2012, 82)

Terminological patterns

A survey of appellations and definitions featured in publications focused on ITr (listed in Appendix 1 in Pięta 2017, in this issue) made it possible to discern the following patterns with regard to English-language publications:

– "indirect translation" has gained ground against other competing designations for both the process and the ultimate TT;[2] interestingly, this trend runs counter to the preferences indicated in most dictionaries, handbooks and encyclopaedias of translation and TS written in English[3]
– when referring to the process and the ultimate TT, native speakers of Iberian languages (Penas Ibáñez 2015; Zubillaga Gomez 2015) tend to opt for indirect translation (a calque from e.g. the Catalan *traducció indirecta*). The same can be said for English native speakers (Landers 2001; Brodie 2012)
– when referring to the process, publications featuring Chinese and Japanese languages as the ultimate SL or TL often opt for "relay (translation)" (Xu 1998; Chengzhou 2001; St André 2010)
– "mediated translation" (after e.g. the Portuguese *tradução mediada*) is predominantly used (with reference to the process and the ultimate TT) in publications featuring Iberian languages as the ultimate SL or TL (Coll-Vinent 1998; Linder 2014)
– when referring to the process, publications dealing with both oral and written translation usually favour "relay translation" (modelled on "relay interpreting") (Dollerup 2000; St André 2009)
– publications on audiovisual (Grigaravičiūte and Gottlieb 1999; Vermeulen 2012) and machine translation (Paul and Sumita 2011) frequently favour "pivot translation"
– the use of "retranslation (re-translation)" in the sense of (the subordinate or a hyponym of) ITr appears most frequent in publications dealing with Chinese as the ultimate SL or TL (Bauer 1999; Idema 2003; Heijns 2003; St André 2003; Jianzhong 2003), but is now extremely rare
– initially the term "second-hand translation" tended to be considered as a synonym of ITr (Popovič 1976, 19; Kittel and Frank 1991, 3); "second-hand translation' is now more often used as a hyponym of ITr, co-hyponyms being third-, fourth-hand translation, etc. (Špirk 2014, 132–133)

Of course, since the surveyed list of publications is not exhaustive, further research is needed to test these patterns and perhaps identify more.

Reasons and consequences

From the above discussion the following explanations for terminological instability in ITr research can be discerned:

– what is under scrutiny is not a simple phenomenon given once and for all but rather one that is complex and constantly evolving (thus bound to generate different terms and meanings);

– national/linguistic traditions and school/branch affiliations appear to induce specific terminological preferences;
– definitions are seldom straightforward; and
– terminology is sometimes employed uncritically and inconsistently.

This metalinguistic instability hinders efficient communication between experts from the
same and neighbouring fields, between teachers and students and also between scholars
and practitioners. As such, it may also have contributed to the still rather weak visibility
of ITr research in the TS community, translator training and the translation industry.[4]

Future research avenues with regard to terminology

This survey shows that there are important metalinguistic questions that still require systematic studies. For example,

(a) how has indirect translation been labelled and defined:
   – in different domains of the translation industry (audiovisual, literary, scientific,
   technical translation, etc.) and in neighbouring research fields (book history,
   textual and genetic criticism, etc.); have there been any changes over time; how
   can ITr research benefit from these terms and definitions?
   – by scholars and practitioners using languages other than English; have there been
   any changes over time?
(b) are terminological patterns identified in publications focusing on ITr also verifiable in
TS with different foci?

It is hoped that research following this special issue may bring further answers.

Conceptual issues

If we take a gnosiological path, "indirect translation" is sometimes used in TS with meanings far removed from that considered here: a translation of a translation. For instance,
Gutt (1989) uses this label to denote a translation that does not aim at interpretative
resemblance to the ST (Pym 2011, 80). ITr is also used to designate a group of strategies
described in Vinay and Darbelnet (1958) and applied when the structural/conceptual
elements of the SL cannot be translated without altering meaning or upsetting the gram-
matical/stylistic elements of the TL (e.g. Newmark 1991, 9). Presently, however, a far more
recurrent designation to describe this notion is "oblique translation" (Vinay and Darbelnet
1995, 31). Finally, the appellation is sometimes used to describe work into the translator's
non-native languages. This happens mostly in English publications by Spanish-native
speakers (e.g. Mira Rueda 2015) although it is much more commonly designated as
"inverse" or "L2" translation (e.g. Pym 2011, 84).

However, even when ITr (or other terms listed in Table 1) is used with the meaning
analogous to that proposed here one cannot help but notice significant discrepancies.

Defining ITr

Probably the most quoted definition is that of Kittel and Frank (1991, 3): ITr is "based on a source (or sources) which is itself a translation into a language other than the language of the original, or the target language". Gambier (1994, 2003) defines it, in a nutshell, as a translation of a translation whereas for Toury (2012, 82) it involves "translating from languages other than the ultimate SLs". Pym's more recent formulation (2011, 80) states that ITr amounts to

> the historical process of translation from an intermediary version. For example, Poe was translated into French by Baudelaire, then from French into Spanish by a number of poets. The Spanish versions would then be called "indirect translations", and the first translation, into French, could then logically be called a "direct translation".

The definitions by Kittel and Frank and by Pym stress that ITr, even if taken at its simplest in terms of number of languages, tends to involve (a) one ST, in one SL (respectively the ultimate ST and the ultimate SL; see next section) and one source culture; then (b) a first translated text in a second language (a mediating text and a mediating language; see "Terminological Discrepancies" below) and within a second national culture; and then (c) a second translated text in a third language (the ultimate TT and the ultimate TL; see "Terminological Discrepancies"), located within a third national culture. To a certain extent, the constellation of both concepts and terms used in the study of ITr suggest that actual communicative situations may be rather more complex. Reality tends to involve one or more texts in the ultimate SL, one or more texts in a mediating language, one or more texts in several mediating languages, and sometimes mediating texts in the ultimate TL, too. However, some of the above-cited definitions explicitly exclude this possibility. Additionally, both Gambier (1994, 2003) and Toury (2012) do not make this definition depend upon the use of three different languages, thereby making it possible to consider, for example, only two languages in defining this phenomenon, but several mediating agents, texts and processes.

More transparent designations for the various subtypes of ITr phenomena could be: (a) direct vs. indirect translation (using the ultimate ST[s] vs. using mediating STs); (b) compilative ITr (using more than one mediating text); (c) mixed ITr (using both the ultimate ST and mediating text[s]); and (d) hidden or open ITr (whether camouflaged as such or openly and explicitly presented as an ITr).

In order to describe, understand and explain the phenomenon of ITr it appears useful to distinguish *several types of indirectness*, depending on

(a) the number and type of mediating texts involved in the process (one or more);
(b) the number of intervening languages (one or more) and their choice – involving the use of only one mediating language vs. the use of more than one mediating language and/or the ultimate SL, one or more mediating language(s), and the ultimate TL;
(c) the degree *of indirectness* (second-hand, third-hand …);
(d) the *presentation of indirectness* (either hidden or open); and
(e) the *status of indirectness* (which for research purposes can be either proven or only presumed).

Regarding the *type of intervening texts*, research might benefit from distinguishing these according to: (a) their language (ultimate ST vs. mediating text vs. ultimate TT); (b) their importance or role in the translation process (primary vs. secondary); and (c) the frequency of their use during the translation process (permanent vs. occasional use); and also their *intended receiver* (public texts, i.e. for wider readership vs. private texts, designed for use by the translator only).

As for the *intervening languages*, research may move forward with a clear identification of both the role played by languages within the translation process, and their status within a world or regional system of translation as suggested by Casanova (2004) or by Heilbron (1999, 2010). Accordingly, one might first distinguish between the ultimate SL, mediating languages and the ultimate TL; and, secondly, analyse these in terms of such categories as dominated/(semi-)peripheral languages(s) vs. dominant/(hyper)central language(s). Most importantly, such an identification might allow for the development of not only descriptive studies of ITr, but also descriptive-explanatory or, in the long run, even predictive studies.

Definitions differ in terms of the number of languages involved. Hence, they may be grouped as follows: (a) those whereby the number of languages is not imposed (e.g. Gambier 1994, 413); (b) those whereby ITr involves *(at least) three* languages, thus making it impossible to consider, for example, back-translation (L1>L2>L1), interlingual translation of intralingual modernization (L1>L1>L2) or retranslation (L1>L2>L2) as ITr (Edström 1991; Bauer 1999; Landers 2001; St André 2009); and (c) those whereby ITr involves *at least two* languages, thus making it possible to consider the abovementioned practices as ITr (Toury 1988, 139; 2012, 82).

Definitions also differ in terms of the relationship between the mediating language, ultimate SL and ultimate TL. Some definitions impose no restrictions as to this relationship (Gambier 1994, 413); others stress that the *mediating language differs from both the ultimate SL and the ultimate TL*, thus making it impossible to consider retranslation or interlingual translation of intralingual modernization as ITr, but possible to consider back-translation as ITr (Kittel and Frank 1991, 3); still others point out that *the mediating language differs from the ultimate SL*, thus making it impossible to consider interlingual translation of intralingual modernization as ITr, but possible to consider back-translation and retranslation as ITr (Toury 2012, 82); whereas other definitions stress that *the mediating language differs from the ultimate TL*, thus making it impossible to consider retranslation as ITr, but possible to consider back-translation and interlingual translation of intralingual modernization as ITr (Toury 1988, 139).

Another important variable is the profile of the mediating text's intended receiver. According to this criterion, the existing definitions can be grouped into those whereby (a) no restrictions are imposed (Gambier 1994, 413); (b) the mediating text is intended only for the *translator working from the mediating text* (Dollerup 2000, 19); or (c) the mediating text is intended for a *wider audience; for example, published* (ibid.).

By now it should be clear that the definition suggested here represents a particularly flexible inclusive approach, as it does not impose restrictions regarding any of the above-mentioned variables. As such, when compared to definitions that are restrictive in their coverage, this approach seems more likely to reflect and keep up with the complex and fast-evolving practice of ITr. It thus seems a more convenient entry point for the launching of this still undertheorized field of research from a scientific basis. An additional advantage is that the definition of ITr as a translation of a translation is clear and concise (thus avoiding ambiguous interpretations) and builds on an existing proposal (thereby helping to optimize current definitions and control their excessive proliferation). However, it is also recognized that such a radically open approach may lead to the questioning of ITr as an autonomous concept given that such a degree of flexibility may raise the problem as to where exactly ITr ends and, for example, retranslation begins.

Towards a classification

In this introduction, we accordingly suggest a classification system, based on three variables:

(a) the number of intervening texts;
(b) the number of intervening languages; and
(c) the choice of intervening languages.

The combination of these criteria allows for the identification of 10 categories, which may be identified by jointly using these labels: direct, indirect, compilative or mixed translation, as shown in Table 5.

Additionally, when subcategorizing indirectness, the following variables appear potentially relevant:

(a) the *subcategory of indirectness* (exposed and hidden ITrs [and checking (exposed) direct translations]);
(b) the *degree of indirectness of the translation process* (second-hand, third-hand translation, etc.);
(c) the *degree of indirectness of the proofreading process and editing process*;
(d) the *mediating language(s)* (the number of languages/cultures involved and their statuses);
(e) the *text-type* (literary [fiction, poetry, drama] or non-literary [LSP ...]; the genre [novel, sonnet]; the mode [written, oral]; the medium [internet, smartphone, TV, printed media, manuscript, volume, periodical], etc.);
(f) the *participants* (author, translator, publisher, editor, proofreader, intended reader and their profiles [commissioning procedure, initiative by publisher vs. translator; status in source culture vs. mediating cultures]);
(g) the *setting* (time and place of publication);
(h) the *intercultural relations* (the existence of non-existence of diplomatic relations between countries, ideological and political affinities between regimes [and censorship], translator training programmes, language teaching programmes, international book fairs, international prizes, etc.); and
(i) the *degree of tolerance towards indirectness* (a greater tolerance [correlate to a higher number of exposed/open ITr] or a lower tolerance [correlate to a higher number of direct translations, exposed/open direct translations, and/or hidden ITrs]).

Open conceptual issues

Open conceptual issues still remain for research to address. The following can be identified as among the most relevant: is the number of languages to be the main criterion for ITr?

Table 5. Tentative classification of ITr.

Texts	Languages	Languages and texts	Classification of process and ultimate TT
1 ultimate ST	1 language	1 ultimate SL text 1 mediating language text 1 ultimate TL text	1. Direct translation 2. ITr (mediating language-mediated) 3. ITr (ultimate TL-mediated)? Or retranslation?
n intervening texts = **compilative**	1 language / n texts	n ultimate SL texts n mediating language texts n ultimate TL texts	4. Compilative direct translation 5. Compilative ITr (mediating language-mediated) 6. Compilative ITr (ultimate TL-mediated)
	n languages / n texts = **mixed**	ultimate SL + mediating language texts ultimate SL + ultimate TL texts mediating language + ultimate TL texts ultimate SL + mediating language + ultimate TL texts	7. Compilative mixed direct and ITr (mediating language-mediated) 8. Compilative mixed direct and indirect (ultimate TL-mediated) 9. Compilative mixed indirect (mediating language + ultimate TL-mediated) 10. Compilative mixed direct and indirect (mediating language + ultimate TL-mediated)

What issues are raised by intersemiotic translation? How are we to deal with intralingual translation (a translation for children into Portuguese based on a pre-existing Portuguese version for a different reader): are we to classify it as ITr or as retranslation? Is it possible to develop effective diagrams for representing indirectness, when several sources are possible and/or probable? How can we deal with the difficulty in accessing information (since covertness is frequent due to negative evaluation)? How are we to deal with presumed ITr, when no proof can be produced, no mediating text identified? What are the main trends for indirect literary translation? How do variables correlate? Are such tendencies different for non-literary translation? For different text types?

Methodological issues

For the sake of addressing methodological issues, three preliminary observations should be made. First, in what follows a distinction is made between studies specifically focused on the phenomenon of ITr and historical TS dealing with corpora that comprise TTs which, according to relevant data on the prehistory of their transfer operations, may be classified as ITrs. In other words, there is a plethora of reception studies that deals with ITrs but only a few works on ITr. These tend to adopt narrow definitions and consider ITr to involve one or more mediating language texts (i.e. comprising solely the cases of ITr and Compilative ITr; see Table 5). Secondly, it should be stressed that ITr does not seem to require a methodology of its own vis-à-vis translation history. It does, however, call for the discussion of some important questions that are not posed, or at least not on the same terms, when dealing with direct transfers. Thirdly, it should be clarified that this section is primarily concerned with the historical study of ITr of literary texts. This is because the major part of research on ITr has had a historical slant, as the articles in this special issue show.

Some recent works on ITr deplore the scarcity of research on indirectness, justifying this apparent lack of interest mainly with the low prestige of the practice of indirect translating (Ringmar 2007; St André 2010; Pięta 2014). In general, this appears to be a valid argument: ITr is considered, indeed, an undesirable practice according to translators' professional ethics in given fields of communication. Nonetheless, there seems to be a more decisive reason behind the fact that research on ITr has not yet reached a desirable degree of sophistication. It should be borne in mind that the same paradox – a successful scientific discipline on a phenomenon with a low symbolical capital – was the basis of the constitution of TS as a whole, as Ferreira Duarte eloquently put it (cited by Maia, Pinto, and Pinto 2015, 320).

However, these reasons apparently have more to do with methodological issues regarding the study of ITr. It is a very time-consuming and costly area of research, since it is text-oriented, calls for specific areas of expertise and, to make matters worse, is still far from providing a meaningful bulk of data that could allow transnational patterns, historical multinational trends or even tendencies in supranational behaviour to be discerned. Accordingly, studies on indirectness still need to make a case for themselves.

Identifying ITrs is a very complex process. The research typically begins by hypothesizing on the indirectness of a TT whenever features perceived as indicators of an additional stage of mediation are observed (be it by a third language, according to some definitions; an additional transfer process; or the intervention of additional mediating agents). These features can be displayed on both the paratextual and textual level.

The importance of paratexts in identifying translations has been argued for, for example, in Lambert and van Gorp (1985). Pym (1998, 62) presents a working definition based on the description of paratexts: "[if] a paratext allows different discursive slots for an author and a translator, then the text may be said to be a translation (working definition)". Regarding ITr, suspicions arise if, for example, the researcher identifies discursive slots for not only the ST author and the TT author – that is, the translator – but also a third agent, the author of a mediating text (mostly by means of an explicit reference to a third language). This third entity can be overtly identified or declared in the paratext; this would be the case, for example, of a Portuguese translation of a Polish text bearing the information "translated from English". However, the researcher will frequently be dealing with hidden ITrs, which might also be labelled pseudo-direct translations (ITrs purporting to be direct translations). In this case, the traces of a third agent will be either presented as, for example, prefaces or introductions by a third-language expert on the ultimate ST author or denounced by covert features such as the transliteration of the author's name.

Some textual features may also lead us to hypothesize on the impact of a third language or a third literary repertoire on a particular TT. The consequences of the mediation of a third language's code (Even-Zohar 1990, 50) or poetics (Lefevere 1985, 217) in fictional narrative are frequently traceable through the analysis of macro-textual shifts. For example, eighteenth-century French translations adapted foreign novels to the generic model in line with French taste. In these translations, known as *les belles infidèles*, some chapters were cut and others added so that the TT would comprise all expected topoi, as adventurous episodes with customs and daggers and a happy married ending (van Gorp 1985; Boulogne 2009; Maia 2010). Due to French's hegemonic status in the World Republic of Letters until the mid-twentieth century, these translations were frequently used as mediating texts in the making of different European TTs. The impact of a third language can usually be inferred from micro-textual features symptomatic of negative interference, such as translation errors, syntactic structures, loan words,[5] proper names (in case of fictional writing), etc.

Following such laborious work, a researcher should have a more solid hypothesis of whether or not the TT in question is an ITr. However, the nature and degree of indirectness of a particular TT can be determined only by the identification of the mediating texts and, thus, mediating languages. Hence, both to confirm the indirectness of the TT and determine its degree of indirectness requires even more effort. For this purpose, some of the research tasks include: (a) exploring the translator's biography, such as which foreign languages they use, which books are in their personal library, where they live, whether they know the ST author or other translators of the ultimate ST; (b) collecting data on the book market, such as which translations were best known; which publishers were exporting to the city where the translation was produced; which booksellers were providing foreign-language texts and from which languages; (c) identifying different linguae francae in a particular time and place, bearing in mind that within one country there may be different bridge-languages (e.g. regions near national borders, or literary and cultural associations dedicated to specific foreign contexts).

At this point, the researcher should have short-listed an array of possible STs and mediating languages. The next stage should be comparison of the TT with the possible mediating texts, which ideally should yield descriptive results similar to those pointed out by Boulogne:

> [a] macro-structural and micro-textual comparison of *De geobroeders Karamazov* (1913) with the early French translations of the same source-texts, has shown that this Dutch translation is a remarkable amalgam of two different French translations. About eighty-five percent of the pages are translated from *Les frères Karamazov* (Dostoievksy, 1906), a translation by Wlademir Bienstok and Chales Touquet. The remaining fifteen percent are translated from *Les frères Karamazov* (Dostoievsky, 1888), a polemical translation by Ely Halpévi Kamisly (1858–1936). (Boulogne 2009, 266)

This apparently simple descriptive research task regarding the ultimate TT involved considerable expertise and means. Firstly, such a project depends on the researcher's knowledge of the language(s) of the ultimate ST, potential mediating texts, and ultimate TT, namely, Russian, French German and Dutch; and considerable time and financial means to explore potential mediating texts, namely the pre-existing French and German translations.

As previously argued, study on indirectness especially, yet not exclusively, in the case of literary translation, shares the methodology of translation history. When listing the research questions to be addressed by historical TS, some authors distinguish between translation's external and internal history. External history is "who translated what, how, where, when, for whom and with what effect?" (Pym 1998, 5). Internal history deals with the analysis of the TTs' aesthetic and ideological makeup. To sum up, it is possible to distinguish translation's external and internal history in these terms: the former is "the kind of history to be construed from context" and the latter "the kind of history to be construed from text" (Koster 2002, 24).

In fact, a considerable amount of relevant data on the phenomenon of indirectness has been uncovered by target-oriented projects in the history of literary exchanges between peripheral languages with "what" questions not explicitly concerned with indirectness. To give but three examples: Boulogne (2009) started by asking "which Dostoyevsky's novels were translated into Dutch?"; Pięta (2016) asked "which Polish literary texts were translated into European Portuguese?"; and Špirk (2014) asked "which Czech literary texts were translated in 20th-century Portugal?" As explicitly stated by Pięta (2014, 17), researchers tend to interpret the "how" question as inquiring into the direct or indirect nature of the transfer of the literary products under study.

While theoretically correct to affirm that the choice of ST pertains to the external, contextual, history of translation, it should be made explicit that, as far as methodology is concerned, identifying mediating texts and mediating languages comprises considerable work with texts. It is thus fair to claim that the study of ITr is probably the area, within TS, more closely linked with the traditional practices of close reading as literary criticism or the Spanish *filología* or the renewed area of genetic criticism.

Identifying ITr, mediating texts and mediating languages is very demanding in terms of textual analysis and, thus, time-consuming. This may prove to be one of the reasons preventing translation scholars from studying indirectness. In order to study indirectness as (a) a large-scale phenomenon; (b) a history- and context-bound phenomenon; and (c) a practice governed by translation norms, we still need relevant historical data on "what has been translated indirectly in a certain context".

In every translation history project, the researcher should start by observing the backdrop and moving on to the particular case study, moving from context to text, or from macro to micro (Assis Rosa 2013, 39–40). This is why Pym (1998, 39) argues in favour of compiling lists as the first step in such projects: "little history can be construed from the analysis of isolated translations. Worse, quite superficial history can result from hypotheses that are pumped up after summary testing on just one or two cases."

This is to say that to understand why ITr occurs, relevant data are needed on existing indirect and direct translations in different contexts. However, whereas lists of TTs (both direct and indirect) can and should be extracted from bibliographies and online catalogues, ITrs cannot be listed only in that way. As Ringmar (2007, 7) clearly puts it: "The information in catalogues and bibliographies is mostly based on paratexts on title-pages and consequently as reliable as its sources, which means that it is not always to be trusted."

Because setting up a comprehensive cartography of the historical phenomenon of ITr is not a realistic project for a researcher or even one research team, our present knowledge concerning ITr remains fragmentary and dispersed, based mostly on case studies. For this reason, comprehensive and relevant questions as to "why ITr occurs" can be tackled only by means of hypotheses based on such case studies. Nonetheless, the above-mentioned examples suggest that multiple conclusions concerning different episodes of the history of ITr are scattered within various studies on translation history.

Does this mean we should abandon research in ITr? Most certainly not! ITr can provide relevant data for timely questions and real-life concerns. One of the many questions addressed by ITr is the need for migrant communities in an increasingly globalized world to adopt linguae francae, and the consequences therefrom. In the 2010 volume of the *Handbook of Translation Studies*, Lieven D'hulst meaningfully relocates the study of ITr within research in translation history. In a list of eight research questions (*quis, quid, ubi, quibus auxiliis, cur, quomodo, quando, cuo bono*), ITr is mentioned under the more general research question "ubi"/"where?" (D'hulst 2010, 4). This seems to suggest that the study of ITr may be productive in shedding light upon microcosmopolitan gestures (Cronin 2006) to engage with culturally distant Others[6] – who can sometimes be our next-door neighbours in hybrid global capitals. On the other hand, it may be instrumental in denouncing malign consequences, of the colonizing power of global languages, as the homogenizing role of English translations (Venuti 1995).

The need for process-oriented cognitive studies of indirect translating and translation didactics should be underscored. With the growing number of exchange student programmes, classes of bilingual translation practice increasingly include students from a third linguistic context (e.g. a Chinese student attending a course in English–Portuguese translation at the University of Lisbon). Kussmaul (1991) successfully demonstrated through think-aloud protocols how translating encompasses the different stages of creative processes. It seems that entering the black box of an undergraduate translation student from China in their rendering of a Portuguese text into English, probably bridging the ST and the TT with Mandarin or another Chinese dialect, may produce relevant data that could afterwards be used in curriculum design.

As far as the historical study of indirectness is concerned, an urgent task appears to be to collect the multiple relevant conclusions and hypotheses spread across multiple case studies published in various countries or presented in different universities. This would require the creation of an international research team willing to list and (critically) read works in translation history, the corpora of which deal with ITrs. The data to be thus gathered will hopefully allow for drawing a chronology of the analysed historical episodes and mapping such episodes may enable us to identify explored and unexplored eras and contexts.

ITr is collaborative in nature. So is the research on ITr. Work hard. Work together. This is its most valuable methodological recommendation.

Notes

1. This suggestion is based on a metalinguistic survey of non-English publications listed in Pięta (2017, in this issue) and is in line with comments made by researchers consulted for the purpose of this study, although more systematic research is clearly needed. German seems to be an exception, perhaps due to the long-standing "Göttingen Sonderforschungsbereich: Die literarische Übersetzung – 1985–1997" project, which systematically researched early-modern translations via French into German.

2. This apparent predominance is not recent (it was first identified in 2006 in Ringmar [2007, 3] and reiterated in 2011 in Pięta [2012, 313]) and is also confirmed by the counting of hits obtained in November 2016 from *Bibliography of Translation and Interpreting* (BITRA; Franco 2001) and *Translation Studies Bibliography* (TSB; Gambier and van Doorslaer 2004) (all fields were queried on terms from Table 1; inverted commas were used to assure that the returned hits correspond to exact expressions).

3. From the 10 works consulted only 3 foreground "indirect translation" in dedicated entries (Chan 2004; Classe 2000; Shuttleworth and Cowie 1997). A dedicated entry in Baker and Saldanha (2009) favours "relay", whereas Gambier and van Doorslaer (2010) prefer "relay translation", and Popovič (1976) uses "second-hand translation". Kittel et al. (2004–2011) do not provide a single entry but, as estimated in Schultze (2014), altogether favour "intermediate translation". The index in Malmkjær and Windle (2011) includes only "pivot translation". The remaining works identified here do not include this concept in their list of entries and indexes (Baker and Malmkjaer 1998; Delisle, Lee-Jahnke, and Cormier 1999).

4. For more reasons behind this weak visibility, see, for example, Dollerup (2014) or Pięta and Maia (2015).

5. More on this in Toury (2012) and Hanes (2017).

6. In his speculation on the possible motivations for publishing indirect translations in current times, Ringmar declares that some foreign works are rendered indirectly, because of an absolute lack of target-culture translators competent in a particular source language. He also suggests that "the case of absolute lack is perhaps the least interesting as there is no real choice between indirect and direct translation" (Ringmar 2007). We tend to disagree with Ringmar on this point. Even if there was no translator available to produce a direct

translation, a choice was still made between (indirect) translation and non-translation. In our reading of the phenomenon of indirect translation, the above-mentioned case of an "absolute lack" of translators signals a cosmopolitan openness to distant cultures with which a particular target culture feels a rather urgent need to communicate.

ORCID

Alexandra Assis Rosa ⑩ http://orcid.org/0000-0002-3267-3213
Hanna Pięta ⑩ http://orcid.org/0000-0002-5229-1941
Rita Bueno Maia ⑩ http://orcid.org/0000-0002-9984-1381

References

Assis Rosa, Alexandra. 2013. "The Short Story in English Meets the Portuguese Reader: On the 'External History' of Portuguese Anthologies of Short Stories Translated from English." In *Translation in Anthologies and Collections (19th and 20th Centuries)*, edited by Teresa Seruya, Lieven D'hulst, Alexandra Assis Rosa, and Maria Lin Moniz, 35–56. Amsterdam: John Benjamins.

Baker, Mona, and Kirsten Malmkjaer, eds. 1998. *Routledge Encyclopedia of Translation Studies*. London: Routledge.

Baker, Mona, and Gabriela Saldanha. 2009. *Routledge Encyclopedia of Translation Studies*. 2nd ed. London: Routledge.

Bauer, Wolfgang. 1999. "The Role of Intermediate Languages in Translations from Chinese into German." In *De l'un au multiple. Traductions du chinois vers les langues européennes. Translations from Chinese to European Languages [One into many: Translations from Chinese to European languages]*, edited by Viviane Alleton and Michael Lackner, 19–32. Paris: Éditions de la Maison des Sciences de l'Homme.

Boulogne, Pieter. 2009. "The French Influence in the Early Dutch Reception of F. M. Dostoevsky's Brat' ja Karamazovy: A Case Study." *Babel* 55 (3): 264–284.

Brodie, Geraldine. 2012. "*Plays in Translation on the London Stage: Visibility, Celebrity, Agency and Collaboration*." Unpublished PhD diss., University College London.

Brodie, Geraldine. 2013. "*Indirect Translation in Theatre: Terminology and (In)Visibility*." Paper presented at the 7th Congress of the European Society for Translation Studies, Germersheim, August 29–September 1.

Casanova, Pascale. 2004. *The World Republic of Letters*. Translated by M.B. Debevoise. Harvard: Harvard University Press.

Chan, Sin-wai. 2004. *A Dictionary of Translation Technology*. Hong Kong: Chinese University Press.

Chengzhou, He. 2001. "Chinese Translations of Henrik Ibsen." *Perspectives* 9 (3): 197–214. doi:10.1080/0907676X.2001.9961417.

Classe, Olive, ed. 2000. *Encyclopedia of Literary Translation into English*. London: Fitzroy Dearborn.

Coll-Vinent, Sílvia. 1998. "The French Connection." *The Translator* 4 (2): 207–228. doi:10.1080/13556509.1998.10799020.

Cronin, Michael. 2006. *Translation and Identity*. Oxford: Routledge.

Delisle, Jean, Hannelore Lee-Jahnke, and Monique C. Cormier, eds. 1999. *Terminologie de la traduction/Translation terminology/Terminología de la traducción/Terminologie der Übersetzung*. Amsterdam: John Benjamins.

D'hulst, Lieven. 2010. "Translation History." In *Handbook of Translation Studies*, edited by Yves Gambier and Luc van Doorslaer, 397–405. Amsterdam: John Benjamins.

Dollerup, Cay. 2000. "Relay and Support Translations." In *Translation in Context: Selected Contributions from the EST Congress*, edited by Andrew Chesterman, Natividad Gallardo, and Yves Gambier, 17–26. Amsterdam: John Benjamins.

Dollerup, Cay. 2014. "Relay in Translation." In *Cross-linguistic Interaction: Translation, Contrastive and Cognitive Studies*, edited by Diana Yankova, 21–32. Sofia: St. Kliminent Ohridski University Press. Original edition, http://cay-dollerup.dk/publications.asp.

Edström, Bert. 1991. "The Transmitter Language Problem in Translations from Japanese into Swedish." *Babel* 37 (1): 1–14.

Even-Zohar, Itamar. 1990. "The Position of Translated Literature within the Literary Polysystem." *Polysystem Studies. Special Issue of Poetics Today: International Journal for Theory and Analysis of Literature and Communication* 11 (1) 45–51. http://www.tau.ac.il/~itamarez/works/books/Even-Zohar_1990--Polysystem%20studies.pdf.

Franco, Javier Aixelá, ed. 2001. *Bibliography of Translation and Interpreting*. Alicante: Universidad de Alicante. Accessed November 2016. http://aplicacionesua.cpd.ua.es/tra_int/usu/buscar.asp?idioma=en

Gambier, Yves. 1994. "La retraduction, retour et détour [Retranslation, Revival and Detour]." *Meta: Journal des traducteurs* 39 (3): 413–417. doi:10.7202/002799ar.

Gambier, Yves, and Luc Van Doorslaer. 2004. *Translation Studies Bibliography (TSB)*. Accessed November 2016. http://benjamins.com/online/tsb/

Gambier, Yves. 2003. "Working with Relay: An Old Story and a New Challenge." In *Speaking in Tongues: Language across Contexts and Users*, edited by Luis Pérez González, 47–66. València: Universitat de València.

Gambier, Yves, and Luc van Doorslaer, eds. 2010. *Handbook of Translation Studies*. Amsterdam-Philadelphia: John Benjamins. Online version accessed December 2016, http://www.benjamins.com/online/hts/.

Grigaravičiūte, Ieva, and Henrik Gottlieb. 1999. "Danish Voices, Lithuanian Voice-Over. The mechanics of Non-Synchronous Translation." *Perspectives* 7 (1): 41–80. doi:10.1080/0907676X.1999.9961347.

Gutt, Ernst August. 1989. *"Translation and Relevance."* Unpublished PhD diss., University College London.

Hanes, Vanessa Lopes Lourenço. 2017. "Between Continents: Agatha Christie's Translations as Intercultural Mediators." *Cadernos de Tradução* 37 (1): 208–229.

Heijns, Audrey. 2003. "Chinese Literature in Dutch Translation." *Perspectives* 11 (4): 247–253. doi:10.1080/0907676X.2003.9961478.

Heilbron, Johan. 1999. "Towards a Sociology of Translation: Book Translations as a Cultural World-System." *European Journal of Social Theory* 2 (4): 429–444.

Heilbron, Johan. 2010. "Structure and Dynamics of the World System of Translation." UNESCO, International Symposium 'Translation and Cultural Mediation', February 22–23, 2010. Accessed September 20, 2014. <http://portal.unesco.org/culture/en/files/40619/12684038723Heilbron.pdf/Heilbron.pdf>

Hyung-jin, Lee. 2008. "Survival through Indirect Translation: Pablo Neruda's 'Veinte poemas de amor y una canción desesperada into Korean'." *Journal of Language & Translation* 9 (2): 71–93.

Idema. 2003. "Dutch Translations of Classical Chinese Literature: Against a Tradition of Retranslations." In *One into Many: Translation and the Dissemination of Classical Chinese Literature*, edited by Leo Chan Tak-hung, 213–242. Amsterdam: Rodopi.

Jianzhong, Xu. 2003. "Retranslation: Necessary or Unnecessary." *Babel* 49 (3): 193–202.

Kittel, Harald. 1991. "Vicissitudes of Mediation: The Case of Benjamin Franklin's Autobiography." In *Interculturality and the Historical Study of Literary Translations*, edited by Harald Kittel, and Armin Paul Frank, 25–35. Berlin: Erich Schmidt Verlag.

Kittel, Harald, and Armin Paul Frank. 1991. "Introduction." In *Interculturality and the Historical Study of Literary Translations*, edited by Harald Kittel, and Armin Paul Frank, 3–4. Berlin: Erich Schmidt Verlag.

Kittel, Harald, Armin Paul Frank, Norbert Greiner, Theo Hermans, Werner Koller, José Lambert, Fritz Paul, Juliane House, and Brigitte Schultze, eds. 2004–2011. *Übersetzung, Translation, Traduction: Ein internationals Handbuch zur Übersetzungsforschung. An International Encyclopedia of Translation Studies. Encyclopédie internationale de la recherche sur la traduction (HSK 26.1–3)*. Berlin: Walter de Gruyter.

Koster, Cees. 2002. "The Translator in Between Texts: On the Textual Presence of the Translator as an Issue in the Methodology of Comparative Translation Description." In *Translation Studies: Perspectives on an Emerging Discipline*, edited by Alessandra Riccardi, 24–37. Cambridge: Cambridge University Press.

Kussmaul, Paul. 1991. "Creativity in the Translation Process: Empirical Approaches." In *Translation Studies, the State of the Art: Proceedings from the First James S. Holmes Symposium on Translation Studies*, edited by Kitty M. van Leuven-Zwart, and Ton Naaijkens, 91–101. Amsterdam: Rodopi.

Lambert, José, and Hendrik van Gorp. 1985. "On Describing Translations." In *The Manipulation of Literature*, edited by Theo Hermans, 42–53. New York: Saint Martin's Press.

Landers, Clifford E. 2001. *Literary Translation: A Practical Guide*. Clevedon: Multilingual Matters.

Lefevere, André. 1985. "Why Waste our Time in Rewrites? The Trouble with Interpretation and the Role of Rewriting in an Alternative Paradigm." In *The Manipulation of Literature*, edited by Theo Hermans, 215–235. New York: Saint Martin's Press.

Linder, Daniel. 2014. "Reusing Existing Translations: Mediated Chandler Novels in French and Spanish." *JoSTrans – Journal of Specialized Translation* 22: 57–77.

Maia, Rita Bueno. 2010. "De como o Lázaro de Tormes e o Diabo Coxo entraram em Portugal e de como aí se apresentaram" [Of how Lázaro de Tormes and the Devil upon two sticks entered Portugal and the way the presented themselves]. In *Perfiles de la traducción hispano-portuguesa III*, edited by Xosé Manuel Dasilva, 99–114. Vigo: Editorial Academia del Hispanismo.

Maia, Rita Bueno, Marta Pacheco Pinto, and Sara Ramos Pinto. 2015. "Translation Studies in Portugal and Interview with João Ferreira Duarte." In *How Peripheral Is the Periphery? Translating Portugal Back and Forth: Essays in Honour of João Ferreira Duarte*, edited by Rita Bueno Maia, Marta Pacheco Pinto, and Sara Ramos Pinto, 319–331. Newcastle upon Tyne: Cambridge Scholars.

Malmkjær, Kirsten, and Kevin Windle, eds. 2011. *The Oxford Handbook of Translation Studies*. Oxford: Oxford University Press.

Mira Rueda, Concepción. 2015. "Didactic Suggestions for Teaching General Translation (English-Spanish, Spanish-English)." *Translation Journal*. January. http://translationjournal.net/January-2015/didactic-suggestions-for-teaching-general-translation.html.

Newmark, Peter. 1991. *About Translation*. Clevdon: Multilingual Matters.

Paul, Michael, and Eiichiro Sumita. 2011. "Translation Quality Indicators for Pivot-based Statistical MT." In *Proceedings of the 5th International Joint Conference on Natural Language Processing*, 811–818. Chiang Mai: Asian Federation of Natural Language Processing.

Penas Ibáñez, Beatriz. 2015. "The Role of Indirect Translation in the Ralentization of Cultural Modernization: The Intermediate Role of Hemingway's Early Spanish Translations." *Transfer* 10 (1–2): 51–74.

Pięta, Hanna. 2012. "Patterns in (In)directness: An Exploratory Case Study in the External History of Portuguese Translations of Polish Literature (1855–2010)." *Target* 24 (2): 310–337. doi:10.1075/target.24.2.05pie.

Pięta, Hanna. 2014. "What do (we think) we Know About Indirectness in Literary Translation? A Tentative Review of the State-of-the-Art and Possible Research Avenues." In *Traducció indirecta en la literature catalana*, edited by Ivan Garcia Sala, Diana Sanz Roig, and Bozena Zaboklicka, 15–34. Barcelona: Punctum.

Pięta, Hanna. 2016. "On Translation Between (Semi-)Peripheral Languages: An Overview of the External History of Polish Literature Translated into European Portuguese." *The Translator* 22 (3): 354–377. doi:10.1080/13556509.2016.1163812.

Pięta, Hanna. 2017. "Theoretical, Methodological and Terminological Issues in Researching Indirect Translation: A Critical Annotated Bibliography." *Translation Studies* 10 (2). doi:10.1080/14781700.2017.1285247.

Pięta, Hanna, and Rita Bueno Maia. 2015. "*Integrating Indirect Translation into the Academic Education of Future Generations of Translators across Europe: A Lisbon Model.*" Poster presented at the Translating Europe Forum, Brussels, European Commission, Directorate General for Translation, 29–30 October.

Popovič, Anton. 1976. *Dictionary for the Analysis of Literary Translation*. Edmonton: University of Alberta.

Pym, Anthony. 1998. *Method in Translation History*. Manchester: St. Jerome Publishing.

Pym, Anthony. 2011. "Translation Research Terms: A Tentative Glossary for Moments of Perplexity and Dispute." In *Translation Research Projects 3*, edited by Anthony Pym, 75–100. Tarragona: Intercultural Studies Group.

Ringmar, Martin. 2007. "Roundabouts Routes: Some Remarks on Indirect Translations." In *Selected Papers of the CETRA Research Seminar in Translation Studies 2006*, edited by Francis Mus. Leuven: CETRA. Accessed April 22, 2011. http://www.kuleuven.be/cetra/papers/papers.html

Ringmar, Martin. 2012. "Relay Translation." In *Handbook of Translation Studies*, edited by Yves Gambier, and Luc van Doorslaer, 141–144. Amsterdam: John Benjamins.

Ringmar, Martin. 2015. "Figuring out the Local within the Global: (Sub)systems and Indirect Translation." *Special Issue of IberoSlavica*, 153–170.

Schultze, Brigitte. 2014. "Historical and Systematical Aspects of Indirect Translation in the de Gruyter Handbuch Übersetzung – HSK 26 .1-3: Insight and Impulse to Further Research." *De Gruyter* 59 (4): 507–518.

Shuttleworth, Mark, and Moira Cowie. 1997. *Dictionary of Translation Studies*. Manchester: St. Jerome.

Snell-Hornby, Mary. 2007. "What's in a Name?' On Metalinguistic Confusion in Translation Studies." *Target* 19 (2): 313–325.

St. André, James. 2003. "Retranslation as Argument: Canon Formation, Professionalization, and International Rivalry in 19th Century Sinological Translation." *Cadernos de Tradução* 11 (1): 59–93.

St. André, James. 2009. "Relay." In *Routledge Encyclopedia of Translation Studies*. 2nd ed., edited by Mona Baker and Gabriela Saldanha, 230–232. London: Routledge.

St. André, James. 2010. "Lessons from Chinese History: Translation as a Collaborative and Multistage Process." *TTR : traduction, terminologie, rédaction* 23 (1): 71–94.

Špirk, Jaroslav. 2014. *Censorship, Indirect Translation and Non-translation: The (Fateful) Adventures of Czech Literature in 20th-century Portugal*. Newcastle upon Tyne: Cambridge Scholars Publishing.

Toury, Gideon. 1988. "Translating English Literature via German and Vice Versa: A Symptomatic Reversal in the History of Modern Hebrew Literature." In *Die literarische Übersetzung. Stand und Perspektiven ihrer Erforschung*, edited by Harald Kittel, 139–157. Berlin: Erich Schmidt.

Toury, Gideon. 1995. *Descriptive Translation Studies and beyond*. Amsterdam: Benjamins.

Toury, Gideon. 2012. *Descriptive Translation Studies and Beyond*. Rev. ed. Amsterdam: John Benjamins. Original edition, 1995.

Van Gorp, Hendrik. 1985. "Translation and Literary Genre: The European Picaresque Novel in the 17th and 18th Centuries." In *The Manipulation of Literature: Studies in Literary Translation*, edited by Theo Hermans, 136–149. New York: Saint Martin's Press.

Van Vaerenbergh, Leona. 2007. "Polysemy and Synonymy: Their Management in Translation Studies Dictionaries and in Translator Training: A Case Study." *Target* 19 (2): 235–254.

Venuti, Lawrence. 1995. *The Translator's Invisibility: a History of Translation*. London: Routledge.

Vermeulen, Anna. 2012. "The Impact of Pivot Translation on the Quality of Subtitling." *International Journal of Translation* 23 (2): 119–134.

Vinay, Jean-Paul, and Jean Darbelnet. 1958. *Stylistique comparée du français et de l'anglais*. Paris: Didier.

Vinay, Jean-Paul, and Jean Darbelnet. 1995. *Comparative Stylistics of French and English: A Methodology for Translation*. Translated by Juan C. Sagar and M. J. Hamel. Amsterdam: John Benjamins.

Washbourne, Kelly. 2013. "Nonlinear Narratives: Paths of Indirect and Relay Translation." *Meta: Journal des traducteurs* 58 (3): 607. doi:10.7202/1025054ar.

Xu, Yanhong. 1998. "The Routes of Translation: From Danish into Chinese - a Case Study of Cultural Dissemination." *Perspectives* 6 (1): 9–22. doi:10.1080/0907676x.1998.9961319.

Zubillaga Gomez, Naroa. 2015. "(In)direct Offense: A Comparison of Direct and Indirect Translations of German Offensive Language into Basque." *Perspectives* 23 (4): 1–12. doi:10.1080/0907676X.2015.1069858.

Indirectness in literary translation: Methodological possibilities

Maialen Marin-Lacarta ⓘ

ABSTRACT

Translation scholars have recently become interested in indirectness, a productive concept that stresses hidden dynamics in the process of translation, rendering visible the hierarchies between literatures and the complexities of literary translation. Since the publication of Toury's seminal chapter in 1988, researchers working in various linguistic combinations and historical contexts have paid attention to indirect translation. However, there have been few attempts to reflect how it can be studied and documented. Based on both a review of previous research and the author's study of twentieth-century Chinese literature translations in Spain, this article offers a systematic discussion of the different contributing sources (e.g. bibliographic databases and catalogues; paratexts; book reviews; sources about translators; and sources about contexts and translations) and methods (e.g. translation comparisons and interviews). The strengths and limitations of such sources and methods are assessed, with examples drawn from case studies to illustrate each category. This article also discusses methodological issues and offers valuable guidelines for research design.

Indirect translation (ITr) has facilitated literary transfer in different linguistic and historical contexts since ancient times. One of the best-known examples is the translation of the Bible: as no original source text (ST) has been preserved, modern Bibles are based on other translations such as the Greek-language Septuagint, the Latin Vulgate by St Jerome and the King James Bible (Kittel and Frank 1991, 3; Dollerup 2000, 21; Gambier 2003, 58). Although ITr is often mentioned in passing in translation history research, the topic has only recently received systematic attention.

Gideon Toury (1988, 1995) was among the first to highlight the value of studying ITr in his "Translating English Literature via German – and Vice Versa: A Symptomatic Reversal in the History of Modern Hebrew Literature", later revised and published as "A Lesson from Indirect Translation". Since the publication of this seminal chapter, translation scholars working in various linguistic combinations and historical contexts have paid attention to the ITr of literary texts. Pięta (2012, 311) showed that the number of academic articles on this topic has increased in more recent years, with the publication of at least 13 papers and monographs between 2009 and 2011.

However, although Toury (1995, 130, 134), Ringmar (2007, 7–9) and Pięta (2012, 315–317) have offered some guidelines, there have been few attempts to reflect how ITr can be studied and documented. To address the gap, this article reviews the broader notion of indirectness and its conceptual potential for both translation scholars and comparatists, and then discusses the different sources and methods used to analyse ITr. I focus on what each type of source and method is useful for, assessing their strengths and limitations, and making use of case studies to illustrate each category. Since in most case studies reflections on methodological issues are scarce, I also use examples drawn from my own research on Spanish translations of modern and contemporary Chinese literature.

Indirectness in literary translation: A productive concept

The concept of indirectness acknowledges the role of mediation or intervention in the process of literary translation. Such mediation can be human or textual. Human mediation occurs when various agents intervene in the process of translation and this dimension has received widespread attention in the sociology of translation (see, for example, Milton and Bandia 2009; Khalifa 2014). The textual dimension, which involves the mediation of different texts in the making of a translation, is less well researched. There are different types and degrees of textual indirectness; it may involve the combined use of multiple source-text editions, translations, reprints, retranslations, composite versions, unpublished drafts and so on. Although all these forms are common in translation history, they tend to be hidden and have until recently been neglected by translation scholars and comparatists. Nevertheless, some translatorial phenomena, such as retranslations and more recently ITrs, have received more systematic attention (see, for example, Deane-Cox 2014 and this special issue). We should also bear in mind that there are continuities and interdependencies between different types of indirectness and it is sometimes difficult to distinguish one type from another. The notion of indirectness reflects power relations in a complex way, paying attention to agents, giving visibility to hierarchies between literatures and highlighting the complexities of the process of literary translation. Thus, it is a productive concept that stresses hidden dynamics that have recently become of interest to translation scholars, as outlined below.

In a time when the global circulation of literatures and world literature studies have become popular topics in comparative literature, translation is still often seen as an imperfect product, with little attention paid to the complex processes leading to a translated text. For example, the complexities of translation are defined by some scholars in terms of "problems", "mis-translation" and "linguistic difference", as demonstrated by the publication of the *Dictionary of Untranslatables* (Apter, Lezra, and Wood 2014, vii, xv, x). Other important publications in comparative literature underline the role of translation in the dissemination of world literature, such as *The Longman Anthology of World Literature* (Damrosch and Pike 2009), which includes commentary for each translation; however, the focus of the commentary is on accuracy or, rather, inaccuracy and loss. Translation scholars such as Pym (2007) and more recently Venuti (2016) have highlighted the problems of erasing translation and a lack of methodological coherence in works written or edited by prominent comparatists in the United States such as Apter, Saussy, Damrosch and Wood.[1]

In contrast, certain translation scholars have paid attention to indirectness and have described different typologies or degrees: from pure ITrs – when the translator uses another translation as the source text – to "support translations" – when the translator uses specific passages of other translations (Dollerup 2000) – and "eclectic translations" – when the translator uses several mediating translations, often in different languages (Von Stackelberg 1987). Dollerup (2000, 24) reminds us that there are fascinating possibilities in between, while Washbourne (2013) outlines the possible subtypes in more detail. Other scholars such as Lie (2000) and St André (2008) also stress the porosity of conceptual boundaries between original, translation, adaptation, pseudotranslation, eclectic translation, ITr and other cases throughout translation history. The absence of established terminology and conceptual agreement on ITr can be seen as a reflection of the scant systematic studies of ITr until recently.[2] For the purposes of this article, ITr is taken to be "any translation based on a source (or sources) which is itself a translation into a language other than the language of the original, or the target language" (Kittel and Frank 1991, 3).

To address the fact that indirectness is still overlooked in the study of literary translation, this article outlines methodological guidelines for studying indirectness and, more specifically, ITrs. Every research project needs a customized methodology, so not all these sources are helpful for every project. However, the ideas gathered in this article should prove a source of inspiration for the design of appropriate methodologies in ITr research.

Sources and methods

Various sources and methods can be used to study ITrs, including bibliographic databases, catalogues, paratextual elements (e.g. the cover, the copyright page, the title, the preface and notes), book reviews,[3] sources about translators, sources about historical and sociocultural contexts and translations, translation comparisons and interviews.

Although most of the sources and methods discussed below are also used in the study of general translation history, ITr researchers deal with specific issues. Many studies of translation history do not consider indirectness; they may focus on what has been translated, when, why, by whom, or for whom, but without necessarily examining the mediated nature of translations. Sources present particular challenges in ITr research because they tend to hide indirectness, meaning that information must be mined from various sources to determine whether a translation is direct or indirect. The triangulation of results is therefore especially important in ITr research. The hidden nature of textual indirectness is connected to the negative vision of ITr as a "necessary evil" instead of a common phenomenon that is worth studying.[4]

The article pays special attention to how these sources contribute to the study of ITr. As Toury (1995, 129–130) argued, the interest in studying ITr is "not as an issue in itself, but as a *juncture where systematic relationships and historically determined norms intersect and correlate*" (emphasis in the original). That is why ITr is usually researched in relation to direct translation (DTr) rather than in isolation. Like other translatorial phenomena, ITr demonstrates the complexity of translation and literary reception, as translation is rarely a simple operation in which a single ST is translated into a target text (TT) by only one person. More than one person may be involved in the translation, or there is more than one ST, or the ST is the translation of another text, to name but a few possibilities.

Bibliographic databases and catalogues

Consulting bibliographic databases to establish a corpus of translations is a common practice for translation history researchers. Regardless of the scope of a project – translations of a given author, a given period or a literary genre – those focusing on ITr pay special attention to the type of translation and try to distinguish DTrs from ITrs in their first stages.

However, data related to type of translation are often unreliable, especially in the case of hidden ITrs, or "work presented in such a way that the information included on the credit page will lead readers to believe the book has been translated directly" (Marin-Lacarta 2012b, 1). In such cases, the title of the ST and the name of the TT translator often appear in the paratext, but with no indication of any other translator or any mediating text (MT) or mediating language (ML). The more numerous the hidden ITrs, the more inaccurate are the results of searches conducted in bibliographic databases for the type of translation.

Index Translationum, a database used to establish flows of translations, was initiated in 1932 under the auspices of the International Committee on Intellectual Cooperation and, after a period of inactivity (1940–48), relaunched by UNESCO in 1948 (Bokobza and Sapiro 2009). It is available online for translations published between 1979 and 2009; references registered before 1979 can be consulted in the print version. Its main disadvantage is the unavailability and unreliability of data. This has been highlighted by several researchers, such as Šajkevič (1992), Heilbron and Sapiro (2008), Poupaud, Pym, and Torres Simón (2009) and Pięta (2010). Other problems include a lack of distinction between first editions, later editions and reprints (Bokobza and Sapiro 2009) and the limitation of search options; for example, there is no search field for the country of the ST (Poupaud, Pym, and Torres Simón 2009, 271). In particular, there is insufficient data for translations published outside the United Nations member states (ibid., 269; St André 2009, 133). However, most researchers agree that the *Index Translationum* can be used tentatively to sketch large-scale flows, although other sources are necessary when developing complex hypotheses.

Based on my own study (Marin-Lacarta 2012a), the *Index Translationum* presents the following problems for ITr research.

- Hidden ITrs are included as if they were DTrs, probably because the information included in the database is based on the copyright page of the translation. For instance, Lu Wenfu's *El gourmet: vida y pasión de un gastrónomo chino* is listed as a translation from Chinese, as the copyright page of the translation mentions only the original Chinese title in *pinyin*: *Meishijia*. However, a comparison of the Chinese original with the French translation, in addition to the biography of the translator, proves that this translation was done via French. Other examples include Lao She's *Historia de mi vida*, Yan Lianke's *Servir al pueblo* and Mo Yan's *Grandes pechos amplias caderas*.
- Some marked ITrs are included as if they were DTrs. This is less common than the previous error. For example, Jiang Rong's *Tótem lobo* can be considered a marked ITr because the copyright page indicates both the Chinese original title and English title,

but the *Index Translationum* lists this translation as a DTr from Chinese. In contrast, in certain other cases where the copyright page includes the same information, such as *Luna creciente* by Wang Tongzhao et al., the translation is listed as done from English.

- Marked ITrs are sometimes excluded from the list of results. The *Index Translationum* includes the search fields "source language" and "target language", which means that some ITrs can only be found if the ML is indicated as the "source language". For example, if we look for literary translations from Chinese into Spanish, Wang Anyi's *Baotown* and Li Bihua's *Adiós a mi concubina* are not included in the results because the *Index* indicates English as their source language. In contrast, Chinese is considered the source language of other marked ITrs, such as Hong Ying's *Hija del río*, Xu Xing's *Aventuras y desventuras de un pícaro chino* and Alai's *Las amapolas del emperador*. In these latter cases, the language of the original text, the ML and the target language appear in the results.

These problems show that ITrs are often categorized as DTrs or excluded from lists of translations. This is also reflected in the way ITrs have been overlooked in academia: they are sometimes included as part of DTrs (without considering the existence of an MT) or, alternatively, excluded from the history of translations because they are indirect, and therefore considered neither part of the history of translations nor part of the reception of a literature.

Other databases that ITr and translation history researchers consult include national library catalogues, book publishing professional catalogues, publishers' catalogues and commercial catalogues. To give some examples, for translations in French, Bokobza and Sapiro (2009) and Poupaud, Pym, and Torres Simón (2009) used Electre (a professional catalogue created by the Cercle de la Librairie), and the catalogue of the Bibliothèque Nationale de France. For translations of Danish literature in Chinese, Xu (1998) consulted the catalogue of the Danish National Library. For translations in Portuguese, Pięta (2010) used 10 bibliographic sources, including online library catalogues, manual catalogues and reference books. For translations in Spanish, I used the catalogue of the Biblioteca Nacional de España and the ISBN catalogue (Marin-Lacarta 2012a).

Bibliographic databases are useful for establishing an initial list of translations and for trying to identify the type of translation (DTr or ITr), the ML and the MT. Other sources must be used to verify the type of translation (direct or indirect) and complete the list. The most important limitation of the use of bibliographic databases and catalogues is a lack of comprehensive and reliable data. In relation to this, Poupaud, Pym, and Torres Simón (2009) argue that there is no such thing as comprehensiveness in translation history because translations are everywhere and one cannot study them all, which means that we apply our own filters to limit the scope of a project. It is also important to mention that the search for translations (both direct and indirect) in literary magazines is more difficult, as information about the content of literary magazines is not included in bibliographic databases. Archival research is therefore arduous and unlikely to be exhaustive.

The paratext

After establishing a preliminary list of translations, an examination of paratextual elements of translations (such as covers, copyright pages, titles, prefaces and notes) is useful for at least five reasons: (1) to identify or rectify the type of translation, ML and MT; (2) to examine attitudes towards ITr; (3) to provide information about the reasons for ITr; (4) to help study the image and reception of a foreign literature and, more importantly, the role played by mediation in creating that image; and (5) to provide information about translators' views on translations, which are useful for examining the effects of ITr on the TT, and on attitudes towards ITr, MLs and MTs. One of the obstacles when collecting this type of data is that some of the editions that the researcher needs to consult might be difficult or impossible to find. Accessing special library collections, private collections or even looking for old editions in second-hand bookstores might be necessary in certain cases.

The following information can be found in different parts of a paratext: the name of the translator of the MT, the name of the translator of the TT, the title of the ST, the title of the MT, the language of the MT and the type of translation. The title of the ST and the name of the translator of the TT appear more often, and the other fields vary. The information found in the paratext can be incomplete and even misleading. For example, although the title of the ST may appear on the copyright page, this does not necessarily mean it is a DTr.

The cover, copyright page, title, preface or introduction and annotations can provide useful information in a more or less straightforward way. For example, Ringmar (2007) draws attention to the title of the Swedish translation of the Finnish detective novel *Kuka murhasi rouva Skrofin?* [Who killed Mrs Scrof?] by Mika Waltari. The Swedish translation changes the name of the victim to "Kroll" (*Vem mördade fru Kroll?*). "Kroll" (instead of "Scrof") also appears in the Danish, Norwegian, Icelandic, German and Dutch translations, suggesting that they were translated from the Swedish version.

A useful barometer for checking attitudes towards ITr involves distinguishing hidden ITrs from marked ITrs. In addition to paratextual information, other sources must be consulted to recognize a hidden ITr, as the information on the copyright page of such publications is similar to that of a DTr. Once we conclude that the translation is indirect, the paratext reveals whether it is hidden or marked. Examining the evolution of this process together with the evolution in the number of DTrs and ITrs allows us to study changes in attitudes towards ITr. For example, in the context of modern and contemporary Chinese literature translated in Spain, 14 DTrs and 10 ITrs were published between 1978 and 2000, and only 2 of the ITrs were hidden. In contrast, between 2001 and 2010, the number of ITrs increased dramatically, with 19 DTrs and 31 ITrs published. Moreover, hidden ITrs were much more numerous: 17 ITrs were hidden and 14 were marked (Marin-Lacarta 2012b). This trend partly contradicts Toury's (1995, 33) prediction that the tolerance of and recourse to ITr would diminish "as the concept of translation changed, and in direct proportion to a growing emphasis on the reconstruction of the source-text features". The data show that the number of Chinese literature ITrs has not diminished in Spain, although the growing number of hidden ITrs may indicate that ITrs are becoming less tolerated.

Considering the reasons and factors that promote ITr, a preface can sometimes help us understand the conditions under which a translation was published. For example, in the preface of the translation of Mao Zedong's poetry anthology entitled *Mao Tsé-Tung*, the publisher explains why the poems were not translated from Chinese and why the decision was made to translate them instead from Italian:

[P]or falta de traductores con un conocimiento suficiente tanto del chino como del español, y convencidos por otro lado de que la traducción al italiano que sobre dichos poemas ha hecho Girolamo Mancuso superaba, con mucho, a todas las precedentes en distintos idiomas, dado su respeto hacia el sentido épico, cultural, didáctico incluso, poético de los poemas en su versión original, la elegimos para, una vez traducida al español, darla a conocer a nuestros lectores. (Moravia and Mancuso 1975, 67)

[(D)ue to a lack of translators with sufficient knowledge of both Chinese and Spanish, and convinced that Girolamo Mancuso's Italian translation of the poems was greatly superior to previous translations in other languages owing to his respect for the poems' epical, cultural, even didactic and poetic meaning in their original version, this was the version – once translated into Spanish – we chose to circulate among our readers.] (My translation)

The preface can thus be helpful for understanding the publication context, the reasons behind an ITr and the preference for a certain MT.

As Gérard Genette (1987, 7–8) argued, a paratext constitutes a threshold or a vestibule the reader may decide to cross after visiting. It offers a space of not only transition but also transaction, as it has an action, a strategy and an influence on the public. By creating a concrete meaning, it enhances a possible interpretation of the text. Hence, paratextual elements are important in studying the image of a foreign literature. At the same time, paratexts reflect the criteria that critics and publishers apply when assessing and publishing a literary work. In the case of ITrs, the image disseminated by the paratext is shaped by the MT and, more generally, by the mediating culture. The title, the image chosen for the front cover and the way the literary work is described on the back cover or in the preface each privilege a given interpretation of a literary work.

The indirectness or mediation of other literary systems in the reception of a literary work is visible in not only the translation, but also paratextual elements. As I have shown elsewhere, the Spanish back covers of the ITrs of Mo Yan's work are similar to their English back covers (Marin-Lacarta 2014). For example, 40% of the text on the back cover of Mo Yan's *Grandes pechos, amplias caderas* comes from the English back cover. This example shows that the image of the literary work is very often influenced by the image transmitted by the MT and its paratext.[5]

Finally, translators' prefaces and footnotes can provide information about the stances of translators and their views on translation. This is especially helpful if we are interested in critically assessing an ITr by comparing the associated ST, MT and TT. Attitudes towards ITr and the associated ML and MT can also be found in prefaces. For example, Graeber (1991) shows that a group of eighteenth-century German translators who rendered English literature from French versions used their prefaces to criticize both the French language and the methods adopted by French translators.

Book reviews

If bibliographic databases and the paratext cannot provide reliable information about the type of translation, then book reviews cannot help either. In this case, we must resort to the biography of the translator; a comparison of the translations; or interviews with translators, editors and publishers. However, book reviews can be helpful in analysing (1) attitudes towards ITr and (2) effects of ITr on the reception of the translation.

Attitudes towards ITr can be measured by examining the paratext and establishing whether ITrs are marked or hidden. They can also be measured by examining book reviews. After using the information in the paratext to establish that an ITr is marked, we often discover that it is hidden in reviews, indicating intolerance or indifference towards ITr. In addition, the (in)visibility of the translator can be assessed: very few reviews mention the name of the translator of the ST, indicating only the translator of the MT; some do not mention the translator at all (Marin-Lacarta 2012a). This can be considered a limitation of this type of source, but is also a reflection of the importance attributed to translation in the receiving society and historical context.

More importantly, reviews are a valuable source for examining how a literary work is presented to readers. In the case of ITrs, they also bear traces of the mediation of other translations; that is, the indirectness of the reception of a literary work is also visible. For instance, the increasing mediation of anglophone and francophone literary systems in the reception of modern and contemporary Chinese literature in Spain influences not only the number of ITrs, but also the content of reviews of Spanish translations (Marin-Lacarta 2012a, 2013).

A review of the Spanish translation of *Big Breasts and Wide Hips*, translated by Mariano Peyrou from Howard Goldblatt's English version, is a suitable example. Elena Mengual's review, which appeared in *El Mundo* on 4 August 2007, is entitled "Mo Yan, el 'Kafka chino', publica en España 'Grandes pechos amplias caderas' " [Mo Yan, the "Chinese Kafka" publishes *Big Breasts and Wide Hips* in Spain]. It repeats ideas that appear in the press release distributed by the publisher, which is based on the English back cover (Marin-Lacarta 2012a), and thus many elements of this review can also be found on the back covers of the English paperback and hardback editions, such as a description of Mo Yan as the "Chinese Kafka"; comparisons between Mo Yan and Kundera, García Márquez and Faulkner; and descriptions of the book as an epic novel, a tribute to women and a depiction of twentieth-century China. This example shows that the indirectness of the reception influences the Spanish paratext and press release, which subsequently influence the book review.

Sources about translators

Collecting information about the backgrounds of translators is helpful for identifying the type of translation, ML and MT and for analysing the effects of the MT on the TT.

Information about the TT translator helps narrow down the ML and rectify information collected from bibliographic databases or the paratext. For example, the copyright page of Mo Yan's *La vida y la muerte me están desgastando* indicates that the ST is in Chinese ("título original: *Shengsi pilao*"), and the name of only one translator (Carlos Ossés) appears, suggesting that it is a DTr. However, if we examine some information on the translator by checking his translations in the Spanish ISBN database and consulting his CV (available online), we discover that he is an English translator, which suggests that the translation is a hidden ITr. Comparing the TT with the English MT is then necessary to verify this hypothesis, a task made feasible by the fact that there is only one English translation of the novel. In other cases, identifying the MT can be difficult. For example, Sergio Pitol translated *Diario de un loco* by Lu Xun. Based on biographical data found in reference literature by authors such as Fernández de Alba (1998, 122–

125) and Herralde (2000, 55), we know that Pitol translated from English. However, finding the MT of the three short stories included in this book is a "probabilistic" task, as Lu Xun's short stories have been translated many times.[6] It may even be impossible when the original no longer exists (Ringmar 2007, 6).

One of the questions addressed by ITr researchers is the effect of ITr on the TT, which necessitates comparing the MT and TT. Collecting information about the translators of the MT and TT is a useful initial step and, as suggested by Berman (1995, 73–75), it is important to take the translator's stance (*position traductive*) into account. The backgrounds of translators, such as their working languages, their professional activity (i.e. whether they also teach or write), the authors and works they have translated and whether they have written about their views on translation, can help us understand their stances. Archival research such as looking for a translator's correspondence may be useful in some contexts, but access to this type of information can be difficult. ITrs complicate the critic's role, as there are at least two translators and therefore two stances and two different projects. Nevertheless, both translation projects must be considered, and the project of the first translator obviously influences the second translation. We could say that an ITr hides two translation projects.

Sources about contexts and translations

As obvious as it may seem, it is worth stressing that translation history must pay attention to the specific context in which a translation is produced, which is why it is necessary to use a range of secondary sources to gain knowledge about the context and to understand the way ITr was practised and perceived at the time. Other researchers' data about the MT and the TT and about the historical and sociocultural context of publication of both translations can be a valuable resource. When the MT is not defined, collecting information about all the possible MTs can be challenging, which is why translation comparison should be conducted beforehand.

Berman (1995, 79–83) refers to the "horizon of the translator" (*l'horizon du traducteur*), a term borrowed from hermeneutics, to stress the importance of considering the linguistic, literary, cultural and historical factors that define the translator's approach and help us understand the decisions made in a translation. A translation's horizon of expectations is defined by what has been translated and how, the history of cultural exchanges between the two cultures and the knowledge of the culture of the ST in the culture of the TT (ibid.). When studying ITr, defining the "horizon of the translator" of the MT and TT or, in other words, understanding the context in which the MT and TT were published should help us to conduct a productive analysis of the translations.

For example, in his article about Pan Jiaxun's Chinese translation of Ibsen's plays via English, He Chengzhou (2001) reviews the reception of the translations in China and pays attention to the norms of the time. By answering such questions as how the translation was perceived in China at the time and what kinds of translations were produced, He Chengzhou (ibid.) offers a context in which to analyse the translations. He also refers to secondary sources that reflect the opinion of German critics about these translations. He is then able to contrast and oppose these opinions with his findings.

When analysing the reasons behind ITr, understanding the historical and sociocultural context of a publication is also essential. For instance, Gambier (2003, 59) explains that between 1930 and 1970 Estonian translations of English-language literature were done through the Russian versions. The historical context helps us to understand the changes introduced in these texts, as Russian was the language of censorship at the time. Toledano Buendía (2001) also examines historical and sociocultural contexts to explain the French mediation of English literature translated into Spanish in the nineteenth century. Xu (1998, 12) explains the success and vulgarization of a Danish philosophical text translated from English by describing the sociocultural situation at the time of publication.

Comparing translations

Comparing the TT with different possible MTs and with the corresponding ST can help verify the type of translation and, when the translation is indirect, the ML and MT. Moreover, we can compare the TT with the MT and ST to analyse the effects of ITr on the TT. However, accessing particular editions might be difficult or even impossible in some cases. The linguistic competence of the researcher can also be a limitation if potential MTs are in languages that s/he does not know.

Information in the paratext and bibliographic databases as it relates to the ST and MT is often incomplete or incorrect. Similar omissions, additions, modifications and editing, such as changing the order of paragraphs in the MT and TT, can indicate that the translation was not done directly from the ST. For example, Ringmar (2007, 6) originally thought that the first *Salka Valka* in German was a DTr from Icelandic. He made this assumption based on biographical notes about the translator and a monograph written by a scholar who specialized in the German reception of Icelandic literature. However, when he gained access to the German text, he realized that the translation depended heavily on the Danish version.

Information collected through bibliographic databases, the paratext, translator biographies, interviews and contextual information about cultural exchanges helped Pięta (2012) to establish a list of six MLs and a list of possible MTs in the context of Portuguese translations of Polish literature. She then carried out a macrotextual and microtextual comparison. Pięta (ibid., 316) first paid attention to "title, transliteration of the author's name, translator's notes, preface, chapter division, chapter titles and illustrations". The microtextual comparison was carried out on excerpts corresponding to 20% of the total text, with special attention paid to the "transliteration of names, loanwords, cultural phenomena (e.g. measurements), additions, omissions, substitutions and misunderstandings" (316).

Even when the ML is known, comparative analysis can help to establish the MT. Considering Dostoevsky's Dutch translation of *De gebroeders Karamazow* by Anna Van Gogh-Kaulbach, published in 1913, Boulogne (2009) compares different MTs with the TT to establish which French translation was used. The title page of the third edition states that it was translated from French, and a macrotextual and microtextual comparison showed that the Dutch translation was an amalgam of two French translations.

In all the examples mentioned above the comparison was conducted manually and often considering only part of the translation. Thus, the results are often approximate, especially when the ML is unknown and the researcher must compare many different versions to establish a probabilistic genealogy. Forensic linguistic methods developed to detect plagiarism in literary retranslations could inspire new methodological possibilities in ITr research. In this field, Turell (2005, 2007) identified linguistic derivation between translations using qualitative-quantitative methods. She used qualitative analysis to identify similar semantic and pragmatic structures that are difficult to detect using automatic and quantitative tools (e.g. the use of similar translation strategies such as additions and omissions and similar solutions in the translation of puns, rhetorical figures, rhyme, dialect), and used CopyCatch to add statistical weight to the analysis, identifying percentages of identical vocabulary, vocabulary shared only once, uniqueness in vocabulary, noun and verb phrases shared only once, and identical or similar phrases. Although Turell compared translations in the same language, cross-language plagiarism detection is also possible (see, for example, recent studies by Franco-Salvador, Rosso, and Montes-y-Gómez 2016), and could therefore inspire ITr researchers willing to develop tools to identify MTs and establish degrees of indirectness. This type of research would require accessing possible MTs in different languages and digitizing them. Although the tools developed to detect cross-language plagiarism are not designed to compare translations, they could encourage future research in ITr. Research carried out in the digital humanities could also lead to new methods. For example, the Version Variation Visualization project directed by Cheesman (see Cheesman, Laramee, and Hope 2012) applies digital humanities methods to multiple comparable translations. The prototype software compares 37 German translations of Shakespeare's *Othello*. In addition to the academic application of digital methods, the development of semi-automatic tools combined with qualitative analysis could potentially be applied to cases of legal disagreement, allowing the translator of the MT to prove that his or her translation was used as an ST for another translation. The translator of the MT has the right to receive copyright fees, although they are seldom granted, especially in the case of hidden ITrs.

Many scholars also conduct comparative analyses to assess the effects of the MT on the TT. Ringmar (2007) reminds us that ITr does not necessarily lead to an inferior result. However, he also suggests that it generally increases the distance to the ST. For example, cultural adjustments made in an MT may be irrelevant in a TT, such as omissions or amplifications. Pięta (2014), St André (2010) and Lie (2000) mention the positive consequences of ITr to balance the generally negative views associated with the practice.

Different approaches to comparing the ST, MT and TT can be classified into two groups. The first approach focuses more on meaning, lexical choice, sentence structure or a particular difficulty such as the translation of cultural references, and researchers usually conclude that errors are maintained in the TT. Some examples include Edström (1991), Jiménez Carra (2008) and Ku's (2010) contributions. These researchers are not interested in explaining the reasons behind the decisions taken by the translators of the MT and TT, and thus do not always pay attention to the publication context of the translations or the literary reception in the mediating and target cultures.

The second approach is characterized by a focus on the role of cultural mediation and on explaining the cultural, social and historical reasons behind manipulations of plot, structure, characters, descriptions or even lexical choices and sentence structure. Examples include contributions by Pajares (2000), Toledano Buendía (2001), Rodríguez Espinosa (2001), Boulogne (2009) and Marin-Lacarta (2012a).

Although there are no clear boundaries between these two approaches, the division can be helpful in understanding the different orientations. Edström's (1991) philological analysis is at one end of the continuum (the most linguistically oriented end). Boulogne's

(2009) approach belongs at the other end and is a good example of more culturally oriented research.

Interviews

Interviews with different agents involved in the translation process – including not only publishers and translators, but also literary agents, editors and proofreaders – are a useful source of data for identifying the type of translation, ML and MT and studying the reasons behind ITr, the process of reception and the consequences of ITr on literary reception. For practical reasons, this section is useful only for research performed in the contemporary period. It must be remembered that publishers are not always willing to release information about the publishing process (Pięta 2012, 316) and interviewees can lie, which is why other sources and methods should always be taken into account.

In my study of modern and contemporary Chinese literature translated in Spain, interviews with publishers helped me to identify the type of translation, ML and MT of hidden ITrs, such as Lao She's *Historia de mi vida* (translated from French), and Mo Yan's *Grandes pechos amplias caderas* (translated from English) (Marin-Lacarta 2012a, 256, 260). Interviews with translators were also useful. For example, Ana Herrera Ferrer, who translates from English and French, told me that she translated Yan Lianke's *Servir al pueblo* from French (ibid., 264). Moreover, interviews with publishers and translators also helped me to outline the reasons ITr is practised. These reasons include market factors (deadlines and rates), a dearth of translators and mistrust shown towards translators of Chinese (Marin-Lacarta 2008).[7]

The consequences of ITr are not limited to the influence of the MT in the TT. Indeed, the MT can also influence the paratext and reviews of the TT, meaning that the influence of the MT is palpable in a literary work's reception. As such, going beyond textual analysis and examining the whole process surrounding the translation, from the choice of the text to be translated to the publication of book reviews, can help us to draw conclusions about the effect of intermediaries such as literary agents, book fairs and publishers on the type of translation and reception of a literary work. The back cover and book review of Mo Yan's *Grandes pechos, amplias caderas* illustrate the significance of the influence of the MT, as mentioned previously. In that case, interviews with the Spanish publisher and two editors were essential to understanding the reception process and the way the back cover and press release were written.

My interviews with translators of Chinese literature in Spain also show that the mediation of anglophone and francophone literary systems can be extended to another phase of the translation process: translation revision (Marin-Lacarta 2012a, 298–299). Two interviewees mentioned that their translations, done from Chinese, were revised and modified by the editor after comparing them with the English translation. In both cases, the translators were not informed of the changes until shortly before or even after the translation's publication. An interview with an editor also revealed that the Spanish editor revised another translation, done from Chinese by a Chinese native speaker, by comparing it with the French translation.

Interviews with publishers who have released twentieth-century Chinese literature in Spain also reveal that most of the translations of fiction published between 2001 and 2010 were selected by publishers who did not know any Chinese and who read translations of these novels in other languages, mainly English and French. After deciding to buy the rights to these works, some of these publishers looked for a Chinese translator, and others had the works translated from English or French. This shows that the indirectness of the reception of modern and contemporary Chinese literature in Spain is not limited to ITrs – DTrs are also done after the publication of English and French translations. Most of the STs were selected at international book fairs or through the recommendation of literary agents. This suggests a new hypothesis that I was able to test by focusing on the date of publication of translations published in Spanish, English and French: the homogenization of the publication of contemporary Chinese literature in English, French and Spanish (Marin-Lacarta 2012a, 295–296). The same literary works are being published in different languages and often almost simultaneously.

This homogenization is a consequence of the role played by international literary agents who sell translation rights on a global scale. ITr facilitates these almost simultaneous publications, as it can be done more quickly than DTr (at least in the case of Chinese translations). Interviews with publishers have provided data about the channels of reception of modern and contemporary Chinese literature in Spain, showing that the mediation of anglophone and francophone literary systems happens as early as when the works to be translated are selected by the publisher, for both DTrs and ITrs.

Conclusions

This article has sought to address a gap in the literature by suggesting sources and methods that can help us study ITrs. The scant attention paid to the textual dimension of indirectness in literary translation is partly due to the absence of methodological proposals to serve translation scholars and comparatists. As mentioned previously, although these sources and methods cannot be applied to all research projects in the same way, the present article provides some valuable guidelines for research design.

By identifying the uses of each type of source and method, this article has outlined a number of questions of interest to ITr researchers, such as identifying the degree of indirectness, and in connection to this, identifying MLs (and therefore MTs); analysing patterns related to variables such as languages, text types, time, authors, publishers and translators; examining attitudes towards ITr and MLs; studying ethical issues and reasons behind ITr; analysing the effects of ITr on the TT; researching the influence of ITr on literary reception and, in relation to this, studying the role of literary agents and other intermediaries, the influence of global literary flows, power differences between literatures and the dynamics of canon formation.

The unreliability of certain sources for identifying ITrs, such as bibliographic databases and paratexts, demonstrates the necessity of using other sources and methods (e.g. translator biographies, contextual information, translation comparison and interviews) and triangulating the results.

Special attention has been paid to the translators involved in ITr. Berman's (1995) methodology for translation critique offers a framework for examining the effects of the MT on the TT by paying attention to the translators of both. Berman's (ibid.) concept of the translator's horizon also underscores the importance of considering the specific context in which ITr takes place. ITr research should not overlook either the translators involved or the historical and sociocultural contexts.

It can be enriching to shift the focus away from the translation and pay attention to the whole process of its reception in the local sociocultural context. Analysis of sources such as paratexts and book reviews has proven to be relevant to examining the broader effects of ITr. When ITr is analysed in the contemporary period, sociological methods of inquiry such as interviews with the agents involved in the publication of the translation have also proven to be valuable sources of data, suggesting that ITr should be studied as a socially situated cultural phenomenon.

Notes

1. It is worth mentioning other initiatives led by comparatists that give visibility to the complexities of translation, such as the four-volume *Histoire des traductions en langues française*, edited by Yves Chevrel and Jean-Yves Masson and published by Verdier.
2. For more on the terminology and meanings related to ITr, see studies by Ringmar (2007, 2–3), Marin-Lacarta (2012a, 79–88) and Pięta (2014, 17–18). This article uses the abbreviations ITr, ST, MT, TT, ML and DTr as previously used by Ringmar (2007) and Pięta (2012).
3. Although other authors expand the meaning of paratexts (and, more precisely, epitexts) to book reviews and translator biographies (see, for example, Gil-Bardají, Orero, and Rovira-Esteva 2012), Genette (1987, 14) restricts the term paratext to those elements written by the author or one of his associates, such as the editor. Following Genette, reviews and translators' biographies are not considered paratexts in this article.
4. György Radó (1975, 51), one of the main promoters in the 1960s of writing a universal history of translation, states: "while English, French, Russian or German poetry has usually been translated directly into Dutch, Swedish, Polish or Hungarian, first-rate English, French, Russian or German poet-translators have rarely adapted poetry directly from these languages. Hence the necessity for indirect translation, a *necessary evil*" (my emphasis).
5. See also a study by Perdu Honeyman (2005), who lists the various consequences of ITr in the case of the Spanish translation of *El Kitáb-i-Aqdas* through the English version.
6. I borrow the adjective "probabilistic" to describe the task of finding MTs from Toury (1995, 134), who also highlights its problematic nature.
7. For more on reasons behind ITr, see studies by Ringmar (2007, 2012) and Pięta (2014).

Acknowledgements

I wish to thank Carles Prado-Fonts, Alberto Fuertes, the two anonymous referees and the editors of this special issue for their helpful suggestions.

Disclosure statement

No potential conflict of interest was reported by the author.

ORCID

Maialen Marin-Lacarta ⓘ http://orcid.org/0000-0001-8444-217X

References

Apter, Emily, Jacques Lezra, and Michael Wood. 2014. "Preface." In *Dictionary of Untranslatables: A Philosophical Lexicon*, edited by Barbara Cassin et al., Translated from French, vii–xvi. Princeton: Princeton University Press.

Berman, Antoine. 1995. *Pour une critique des traductions: John Donne*. Paris: Gallimard.

Bokobza, Anaïs, and Gisèle Sapiro. 2009. "L'analyse des flux de traductions et la construction des bases de données." In *Translatio: le marché de la traduction à l'heure de la mondialisation*, edited by Gisèle Sapiro, 45–64. Paris: CNRS.

Boulogne, Pieter. 2009. "The French Influence in the Early Dutch Reception of F.M. Dostoevsky's *Brat'ja Karamazovy*: A Case Study." *Babel* 55 (3): 264–284. doi:10.1075/babel.55.3.04bou.

Cheesman, Tom (Principal Investigator), Robert S. Laramee, and Jonathan Hope. 2012. *Version Variation Visualization* (project funded by the Arts and Humanities Research Council). http://delightedbeauty.org/vvv.

Chengzhou, He. 2001. "Chinese Translations of Henrik Ibsen." *Perspectives: Studies in Translatology* 9 (3): 197–214.

Damrosch, David, and David L. Pike, eds. 2009. *The Longman Anthology of World Literature*. 6 vols. 2nd ed. New York: Longman.

Deane-Cox, Sharon. 2014. *Retranslation: Translation, Literature and Reinterpretation*. London/ New York: Bloomsbury.

Dollerup, Cay. 2000. "Relay and Support Translations." In *Translation in Context: Selected Papers from the EST Congress (Granada 1998)*, edited by Andrew Chesterman, Natividad Gallardo, and Yves Gambier, 17–26. Amsterdam: John Benjamins.

Edström, Bert. 1991. "The Transmitter Language Problem in Translations from Japanese into Swedish." *Babel* 37 (1): 1–14.

Fernández de Alba, Luz. 1998. *Del tañido al arte de la fuga: una lectura crítica de Sergio Pitol* [From ringing to the art of escape: a critical Reading of Sergio Pitol]. Mexico City: Universidad Nacional Autónoma de México.

Franco-Salvador, Marc, Paolo Rosso, and Manuel Montes-y-Gómez. 2016. "A Systematic Study of Knowledge Graph Analysis for Cross-language Plagiarism Detection." *Information Processing & Management* 52 (4): 550–570. doi:10.1016/j.ipm.2015.12.004.

Gambier, Yves. 2003. "Working with Relay: An Old Story and a New Challenge." In *Speaking in Tongues: Language Across Contexts and Users*, edited by Luis Pérez González, 47–66. Valencia: Universidad de Valencia.

Genette, Gérard. 1987. *Seuils*. Paris: Seuil.

Gil-Bardají, Anna, Pilar Orero, and Sara Rovira-Esteva, eds. 2012. *Translation Peripheries: Paratexual Elements in Translation*. Bern: Peter Lang.

Graeber, Wilhelm. 1991. "German Translators of English Fiction and Their French Mediators." In *Interculturality and the Historical Study of Literary Translations*, edited by Harald Kittel and Armin Paul Frank, 5–26. Berlin: Eric Schmidt.

Heilbron, Johan, and Gisèle Sapiro. 2008. "La traduction comme vecteur des échanges culturels internationaux." In *Translatio: le marché de la traduction à l'heure de la mondialisation*, edited by Gisèle Sapiro, 25–44. Paris: CNRS.

Herralde, Jordi. 2000. "Sergio Pitol, editor" [Sergio Pitol, publisher]. In *Sergio Pitol: los territorios del viajero*, edited by José Balza et al., 53–58. Mexico City: Era.

Jiménez Carra, Nieves. 2008. "La traducción indirecta de los *Últimos Días de Pompeya* de Isaac Núñez de Arenas (1848)" [The Indirect Translation of Isaac Nuñez de Arenas' *The Last Days of Pompeii* (1984)]. In *Diez estudios sobre la traducción en la España del siglo XIX*, edited by Juan Jesús Zaro, 121–138. Granada: Atrio.

Khalifa, Abdel Wahab, ed. 2014. *Translators Have their Say? Translation and the Power of Agency.* Zurich: LIT Verlag.

Kittel, Harald, and Armin Paul Frank. 1991. *Interculturality and the Historical Study of Literary Translations.* Berlin: Eric Schmidt.

Ku, Menghsuan. 2010. "Reflexión de la traducción indirecta del chino al español: ejemplo de la traducción de *La vida y la muerte me están desgastando*" [Consideration on the Indirect Translation between Chinese and Spanish: The Translation of *Life and Death Are Wearing Me Out*]. *Confluenze: revista di studi iberoamericani* 2 (1): 197–212.

Lie, Raymond S. C. 2000. "Indirect Translation." In *Encyclopedia of Literary Translation into English*, edited by Olive Classe, 708–709. London: Fitzroy Dearborn.

Marin-Lacarta, Maialen. 2008. "La traducción indirecta de la narrativa china contemporánea al castellano: ¿síndrome o enfermedad?" [Indirect Translation of Contemporary Chinese Narrative Into Spanish: Symptom or Disease?]. 1611 *A Journal of Translation History* 2. http://www.traduccionliteraria.org/1611/art/marin.htm.

Marin-Lacarta, Maialen. 2012a. "Mediación, recepción y marginalidad: las traducciones de literatura china moderna y contemporánea en España" [Mediation, Reception and Marginality: The Translations of Modern and Contemporary Chinese Literature in Spain]. PhD diss., Institut National des Langues et Civilisations Orientales and Universitat Autònoma de Barcelona.

Marin-Lacarta, Maialen. 2012b. "A Brief History of Translations of Modern and Contemporary Chinese Literature in Spain (1949–2009)." 1611 *A Journal of Translation History* 6. http://www.traduccionliteraria.org/1611/art/marin2.htm.

Marin-Lacarta, Maialen. 2013. "La réception de Mo Yan en Espagne: quelques réflexions sur les canaux de diffusion de la littérature chinoise contemporaine." In *La littérature chinoise hors de ses frontières: influences et réceptions croisées*, edited by Angel Pino and Isabelle Rabut, 169–194. Paris: You Feng.

Marin-Lacarta, Maialen. 2014. "Les traductions de Mo Yan en Espagne: une étude sur la médiation des systèmes littéraires anglophone et francophone." In *Traduction et partages: que pensons-nous devoir transmettre?*, edited by Ève de Dampierre et al., 283–293. Bordeaux: Vox Poetica.

Milton, John, and Paul Bandia, eds. 2009. *Agents of Translation*. Amsterdam: John Benjamins. doi:10.1075/btl.81.

Moravia, Alberto, and Girolamo Mancuso. 1975. *Mao Tsé-Tung* [Tutte le poesie, 1972]. Translated by José Palao. Madrid: Júcar.

Pajares, Eterio. 2000. "Literature and Translation: The First Spanish Version of Tom Jones." *Babel* 46 (3): 193–210. doi:10.1075/babel.46.3.02paj.

Perdu Honeyman, Nobel. 2005. "From Arabic to Other Languages through English." In *Less Translated Languages*, edited by Albert Branchadell and Lovell Margaret West, 67–74. Amsterdam: John Benjamins.

Pięta, Hanna. 2010. "À procura de traduções da literatura polaca em Portugal: algumas questões sobre o uso de fontes bibliográficas na história da tradução" [In Search of Translations from Polish Literature in Portugal. Some eemarks on the Use of Bibliographical Sources in Translation History]. *Itinerarios* 11: 121–139.

Pięta, Hanna. 2012. "Patterns in (In)directness: An Exploratory Case Study in the External History of Portuguese Translations of Polish Literature (1855–2010)." *Target* 24 (2): 310–337. doi:10.1075/target.24.2.05pie.

Pięta, Hanna. 2014. "What Do (We Think) We Know About Indirectness in Literary Translation? A Tentative Review of the State-of-the-art and Possible Research Avenues." In *Traducció indirecta en la literatura catalana*, edited by Ivan Garcia Sala, Diana Sanz Roig, and Bożena Zaboklicka, 15–34. Lleida: Punctum.

Poupaud, Sandra, Anthony Pym, and Esther Torres Simón. 2009. "Finding Translations. On the Use of Bibliographical Databases in Translation History." *Meta: Journal des traducteurs* 54 (2): 264–278. doi:10.7202/037680ar.

Pym, Anthony. 2007. "Emily Apter. *The Translation Zone: A New Comparative Literature.*" *Target* 19 (1): 177–182. doi:10.1075/target.19.1.15pym.

Radó, György. 1975. "Indirect Translation." *Babel* 21 (2): 51–59.

Ringmar, Martin. 2007. "'Roundabout Routes': Some Remarks on Indirect Translations." In *Selected Papers of the CETRA Research Seminar in Translation Studies 2006*, edited by Francis Mus. https://www.arts.kuleuven.be/cetra/papers/files/ringmar.pdf.

Ringmar, Martin. 2012. "Relay Translation." In *Handbook of Translation Studies, Vol. 3*, edited by Yves Gambier and Luc van Doorslaer, 141–144. Amsterdam: John Benjamins.

Rodríguez Espinosa, Marcos. 2001. "Ideological Constraints and French Mediation in Hispanic Translated Texts: 1860–1930." *TRANS: revista de traductología*, no. 5: 9–22. http://www.trans.uma.es/trans_05.html.

Šajkevič, Anatolij J. A. 1992. "Bibliometric Analysis of *Index Translationum.*" *Meta: Journal des traducteurs* 37 (1): 67–96. doi:10.7202/004017ar.

St. André, James. 2008. "Relay." In *Routledge Encyclopedia of Translation Studies*, edited by Mona Baker and Gabriela Saldanha, 230–232. London: Routledge.

St. André, James. 2009. "History." In *Routledge Encyclopedia of Translation Studies*, edited by Mona Baker and Gabriela Saldanha, 133–136. London: Routledge.

St. André, James. 2010. "Lessons from Chinese History: Translation as a Collaborative and Multistage Process." *TTR: Traduction, Terminologie, Rédaction* 23 (1): 71–94. doi:10.7202/044929ar.

Toledano Buendía, Carmen. 2001. "Robinson Crusoe naufraga en tierras españolas" [Robinson Crusoe wrecks in Spanish lands]. *Babel* 47 (1): 35–48. doi:10.1075/babel.47.1.05tol.

Toury, Gideon. 1988. "Translating English Literature via German and Vice Versa: A Symptomatic Reversal in the History of Modern Hebrew Literature." In *Die literarische Übersetzung: Stand und Perspektiven ihrer Erforschung*, edited by Harald Kittel, 139–157. Berlin: Erich Schmidt.

Toury, Gideon. 1995. "A Lesson from Indirect Translation." Chap. 7 in *Descriptive Translation Studies and Beyond*. Amsterdam: John Benjamins.

Turell, María Teresa. 2005. "El plagio en la traducción literaria." In *Lingüística forense, lengua y derecho: conceptos, métodos y aplicaciones*, edited by María Teresa Turell, 275–298. Barcelona: Institut Universitari de Lingüística Aplicada, Universitat Pompeu Fabra; Documenta Universitaria.

Turell, María Teresa. 2007. "Plagio y traducción literaria." *Vasos Comunicantes* 37 (1): 43–54.

Venuti, Lawrence. 2016. "Hijacking Translation: How Comp Lit Continues to Suppress Translated Texts." *Boundary 2: an International Journal of Literature and Culture* 43 (2): 179–204. doi:10.1215/01903659-3469952.

Von Stackelberg, Jurgen. 1987. "Eklektisches Übersetzen. Erläutert am Beispiel einer italienischen Übersetzung von Salomon Geßners *Idyllen*" [Eclectic Translation: Illustrated by the Example of the Italian Translation of *Idylls*, by Salomon Gessner]. In *Die literarische Übersetzung: Fallstudien zu ihrer Kulturgeschichte* [Literary translation: Case studies for its cultural history], edited by Brigitte Schultze, 53–62. Berlin: Erich Schmidt.

Washbourne, Kelly. 2013. "Nonlinear Narratives: Paths of Indirect and Relay Translation." *Meta: Journal des traducteurs* 58 (3): 607–625. doi:10.7202/1025054ar.

Xu, Yanhong. 1998. "The Routes of Translation: From Danish into Chinese – A Case Study of Cultural Dissemination." *Perspectives: Studies in Translatology* 6 (1): 9–22. doi:10.1080/0907676X.1998.9961319.

Arguing for indirect translations in twenty-first-century Scandinavia

Cecilia Alvstad

ABSTRACT
The article explores why indirect translation takes place, especially in contexts where policymakers work against it by, for example, not providing translation grants for such translations. The focus is on contemporary Sweden, and the article pays particular attention to arguments expressed in favor of indirect translation in a series of 11 books translated indirectly from Assamese, Bengali, Hindi, Kannada, Malayalam, Marathi, Odia, Tamil or Urdu. It concludes by suggesting that cultural policies with more permissive criteria concerning indirectness of translation could be beneficial.

Introduction

From 2001 to 2009, a series of 11 books was published in Sweden under the name *Indiska biblioteket* (The Indian library). Except for some poems that were originally written in English, all of these 11 volumes comprised translations of translations.[1] The books offered something new to the Swedish target culture as they introduced novels, short stories, poems and a few non-literary prose texts written in Indian languages other than English. None of the many Swedish translators behind these volumes had any proficiency at all in the original source languages of Assamese, Bengali, Hindi, Kannada, Malayalam, Marathi, Odia, Tamil or Urdu. The Swedish translators based their selection and their translations on a combination of published translations and on the information Indian collaborators gave them on site in India and via email. This is accounted for in several of the introductions and epilogues of the Swedish translations (see e.g. Stolpe [2008, 293], and examples further on in this article).

In many ways this book series constitutes an exceptional case. Toury's (1995, 82) preliminary norm referring to translation policy is breached since the choice of texts to be translated is an unusual one. Literary texts from India, originally written in languages other than English, had not been published in Swedish before. The fact that the texts in this context were translated indirectly implies a breach of another of Toury's (ibid., 82) preliminary norms, namely that related to directness. Furthermore, indirect translations in Sweden are typically published in a way that makes it difficult for the non-professional reader to discover that they were not translated directly from the language of the original (see next section for examples). Throughout the series *Indiska biblioteket*, however, the indirectness is not only openly shown, it is advocated. There are forewords, introductions and epilogues in almost every installment and in these the translators and editors explain what they do and how and why they do it. This abundance of translational paratexts means that a third Swedish translation norm is breached since it is rather unusual that translations into Swedish are published with so much paratextual material.

I assume that the breaching of the three norms is interrelated, and in the following will therefore discuss the breach of the directness norm in relation to a series of questions related to how the texts were selected for translation, what audience they seem to cater for and what kind of lack in the target culture they were supposed to fill. With particular attention to how they talk about indirect translation, I will therefore provide a reflexive account of what the editors and translators write in the paratexts. I will also look into the reception of the series in the daily press. The book series in fact received considerable attention, with a total of 67 articles, of which 27 were reviews.[2]

The overarching aim of this article is to better understand why indirect translation takes place, especially in contexts where cultural policies discourage such efforts. By looking at the values these practitioners draw attention to, I believe we might learn something about potential limitations related to mainstream practice, which in this case would be direct translation and hidden or semi-hidden indirect translation.

In order to provide a background for what the translators and editors of *Indiska biblioteket* do and how they and reviewers in Swedish media write about their practice, I will first make some general observations about indirect translation in the Scandinavian context.

Background observations

Present-day cultural policies in Scandinavia clearly favor direct over indirect translation. Only in exceptional cases would it be possible to get a grant for translating via a third language into Danish, Swedish or Norwegian from the relevant Scandinavian state institutions, as eligibility requires that translations must be direct (Danish Arts Foundation 2016), should preferably be direct (Swedish Arts Council 2016b) or only exceptionally can be indirect (Arts Council Norway 2016). These policies mean that it would be almost impossible for indirect translations like those of the book series *Indiska biblioteket* to receive grants from the Swedish Arts Council. The series did receive some financial support but from an entirely different state institution, namely Sweden's development aid agency Sida, which works on behalf of the Swedish parliament and government "with the mission to reduce poverty in the world" (Sida 2016). Thus, the books of this series concern not only the literary field but also that of development aid, which may give rise to a wish or even need (whether perceived or real) to meet specific demands and expectations.

It is also worth noting that conditions are even stricter when it comes to translation from Swedish into other languages. The translation then "must be done directly from Swedish" (Swedish Arts Council 2016a). The implication of this strict policy is that not even translations paid for by the Swedish Arts Council can be considered good enough to base another translation on. This is ironic, especially in the light of recent research suggesting that it is not necessarily possible to tell an indirect from a direct translation using quantitative methods, and that indirect translations can even be closer to the original than the intermediary text that served as a source (Hekkanen 2014, 61–62). Hekkanen explains this result by drawing attention to the fact that indirect translators do not necessarily use the intermediary text as their only source.

While Hekkanen does not display the same negative attitudes toward indirect translations as the Scandinavian grant institutions, it remains possible to find examples of not only grant institutions but also translation scholars who write negatively about indirect translation, notably often in passing when studying a different phenomenon. Tegelberg, for instance, states in an article on retranslation that "as a matter of principle, it is of course desirable for literary translation not to be carried out via an intermediary language" (2011, 86; all translations from Swedish in this article are mine).[3] Tegelberg supposes that it is less common to translate indirectly today than it used to be in the past; scholars outside Scandinavia have also suggested that this is a decreasing phenomenon (e.g. Heilbron 1999, 436). Heilbron points out that a decreasing number of indirect translations would not mean that central languages lose their role as mediators when it comes to translation between peripheral languages, since literary texts written in peripheral languages are dependent on first getting translated into a central language if they are to get translated into other languages.[4]

I agree with Heilbron on this last point, but need to point out that indirect translation is not a practice restricted to the past. Despite the strict rules for grants, a fair amount of indirect translation is currently taking place in, for example, Sweden. To cite a few recent examples, most books by Nobel laureate Orhan Pamuk have been translated into Swedish from versions other than the Turkish original. David Grossman's *Isha Borachat Mi'bsora*, which in English is called *To the End of the Land*, was translated from English rather than Hebrew, while Marlene Van Niekerk's *Agaat* was translated from English and not Afrikaans. This is accounted for on the title pages. Other cases are more covert, such as Kyong-Sook Shin's *Please Look After Mother*, in which the indirectness is more concealed but can be deduced by anyone who knows that the translator does not translate from Korean.[5] It is equally easy to find examples of indirect translations into Norwegian and Danish, though not necessarily of the same books.

I have given these examples to show that the books in *Indiska biblioteket* are not the only indirect translations to appear in present-day Sweden. None of these other translations, however, contains a foreword or epilogue in which the translators or editors argue in favor of the indirect method employed. In these other books, even where the indirectness is acknowledged in very clear terms (which is not always the case), it is done in a discreet manner and on the title page only. The few examples given here show that it would be interesting to study the relative percentages of direct and indirect translations, the degree of overtness about the indirectness, and whether indirect translation is becoming more or less common. In other words, the Swedish book market deserves a study similar to Marin-Lacarta's (2012) about translation from Chinese into Spanish. Marin-Lacarta's study reveals a very interesting change in how works are selected for translation, a change that affects the directness of translation, going from a majority of direct translations in 1978–2000 to a majority of indirect translations in 2001–09. This was related to a change in who took the initiative to translate the books. In the first period, Spanish translators would suggest works to be translated. This practice changed after 2000, when Gao Xingjian was awarded the Nobel Prize in Literature, as publishers instead started to select Chinese works for translation on the basis of the authors' status in the anglophone and French literary systems.

Marin-Lacarta's data are interesting because from them one can conclude that Tegelberg and Heilbron might be wrong in assuming that there presently is a move only away from indirect and toward direct translation. There are also specific moves in the reverse direction. Marin-Lacarta also shows that many of the indirect translations are hidden, in that they are presented as if they were originally written in English (Marin-Lacarta 2012, 3–6). In this respect there is an important difference compared with *Indiska biblioteket*, which actually employs exactly the opposite strategy for which, as I will show below, it would be difficult to imagine a more overt way to address the question of indirectness.

Multiple translatorship and indirect translation in *Indiska biblioteket*

When working on the *Indiska biblioteket* series, the translation agents neither worked alone nor translated directly from the original language, as per the popular image. The 11 books were rather published by means of a collaboration between such agents, none knowing both the original and the target languages. In most cases, the Swedish translators based their translations on a combination of published translations into French, German and Danish along with intermediary texts in English that were produced orally and/or in writing specifically for them as part of this translation project from the Assamese, Bengali, Hindi, Kannada, Malayalam, Marathi, Odia, Tamil or Urdu original texts (see Appendix). In this section I will examine more closely what the agents wrote about their collaboration.

Inspired by Stillinger's (1991) concept of "multiple authorship", Jansen and Wegener (2013, 4) coined the term "multiple translatorship" to highlight how there are always multiple agents involved in the shaping of a translation. In addition to at least one translator, there is an author who may have a say, as well as publishers, editors, copy-editors and so forth. In the reception of the work, reviewers, journalists, librarians and similar agents continue to shape the translation through the diverse ways in which they write about, classify and present literary works.

The *Indiska biblioteket* series involved even more agents than typically. Indian collaborators played important roles in guiding the selection and explaining terms and cultural phenomena. These collaborators guided the selection of texts to be translated with the important limitation that everything had to have been translated previously into English (or German, French and/or a Scandinavian language). Some of the translations had been published in English in India, while others had been published in Great Britain, the United States, France or Germany (see Appendix). Indian collaborators with knowledge of the original language then helped the Swedish translators by explaining words or stylistic features, comparing the published text to the original and/or producing their own translations into English (Sjöström 2001, 161; Stolpe 2008, 293).

Birgitta Wallin, one of the series' two editors and also a translator of some of the texts, writes as follows about the translation policy, the translation method employed and the difficulty of finding translators:

> This anthology is being published as part of the Swedish-Indian translation project's *Indiska biblioteket* book series. In the project we have chosen to translate mostly Indian literature that was written in not English but rather some of the country's many other languages. Daily life in India largely unfolds in these languages, but the literature that is written in for example Gujarati, Malayalam or Odia is seldom to be found outside of the country's borders. The structure of the book market is the largest obstacle, but another reason is that it is not particularly easy to find translators. We have therefore worked according to a method we learned from our Indian friends: we translated by using an English and sometimes also a French or

German version, before revising the translation against the original alongside a person proficient in the original language (in which case another language must serve as a link, which as a rule was English). If this work can be done at a location closely associated with the text's origin, so much the better. (2008, 156–157)

Wallin here explains and justifies how the translation agents worked, and gives credit to the Indian collaborators when it comes to the method involving intermediary translations produced for the Swedish translators. Several of the Swedish agents claim that it would have been difficult or impossible to find translators capable of translating the texts directly (see e.g. Stolpe 2008, 293). As there is no tradition in Sweden for translating Indian literature from languages other than English, this may very well be true, which is confirmed by the list of 35 languages that Swedish literary and non-literary translators who are members of the organization Översättarcentrum (2016) translate from: English is the only Indian language on the list. That the organization has no members who translate from other Indian languages is not to imply that there are no speakers of these languages in Sweden, and so to train such speakers as translators would have been a possibility. This is in fact a path chosen by the Norwegian Association of Literary Translators, which offers courses in literary translation from lesser translated languages. The project is called Flerstemt ("multivoiced") and includes Hindi (Norsk oversetterforening 2016). It is worth noting that the ethical implications of these two choices are quite different. Relevant questions to ask in this context are: who is allowed to translate whom? And which option best serves to increase translations from lesser translated languages?

As for what the Swedish translation agents were seeking, they seem to have searched for texts with literary qualities that could appeal to a wider audience as well as provide Swedish readers with cultural insight and knowledge about India. The following quote from the introduction to Basheer (2008) exemplifies these criteria:

> When we began planning the *Indiska biblioteket* book series ten years ago, we asked Indian friends and colleagues whether they could suggest any writers they thought we should translate. One of the names that came up most frequently was Vaikom Muhammad Basheer.
>
> "What, haven't you read Basheer? But how could you have missed him?"
>
> No matter whether they were a member of the cultural elite or a regular book lover, no matter their age group or linguistic background, people lauded Basheer for his way of describing life and everyday situations, devoid of grammatical or ideological blinders. Basheer, we came to understand, was the friend of his readers, the exegete of the street and the soil, a writer of the people but also a writer's writer.
>
> So, finally, we began reading Basheer. We read his short stories and novellas, whatever was available in English, and we were captivated by his willful style and wistfully humorous texts. They were a challenge to translate, we found out, but certainly something that should be made available to Swedish readers. (Löfström and Wallin 2008, 7)

The poetry anthology *Innan Ganges flyter in i natten* (Before Ganges flows into the night; Löfström and Wallin 2009a) also discusses how languages and texts were selected. Unlike other volumes of the series, this book includes direct translations of Indian poetry originally written in English, together with translations from Hindi and Malayalam. The reason the editors offer for including only 3 languages in this 387-page volume is to give more weight to each section (Löfström and Wallin 2009b, 13). Moreover, the editors describe how they first selected texts in Sweden, but updated this selection when they met in India with their collaborators:

> At the outset, the selection was limited somewhat vaguely to "contemporary" poetry, that is poetry beginning with the advent of modernism sometime during the 1920s. Along with our Indian friends, we set up a preliminary list of 20–25 poets from each language from this time span, and the poems were variously culled from anthologies, book shelves and drawers. Obviously, it was a prerequisite that at least rudimentary English translations were available so that the Swedish translators could gain an impression of the poems.
>
> Next, we began translating the poems on the basis of these English versions, and with our rough Swedish translations in our bags we traveled to India. There, we carefully reviewed the poems with the Indian co-translators, who compared the translations with the original-language texts. During this phase it turned out that certain poets had to be scratched (usually because they quite simply were too difficult to translate, for various reasons), while other names were added, poets that we did not have access to in Sweden. In the end, around 15 poets from each language remained. (Ibid., 13)

The poems in *Innan Ganges flyter in i natten* are presented by language, with a short introduction before each new section by one of the Indian collaborators that places authors and poems in their literary context (Grover 2009; Hasan 2009; Satchidanandan 2009). Not only does this give the anthology a more scholarly feel than the other books in the series, which do not include such introductions, it also underscores that the Indian collaborators' input was not restricted to language skills or cultural knowledge.

The lines above in addition illustrate the degree to which this was indeed a collaborative endeavor, a point also made clear by the many Indian collaborators named in the books, whether on the title page, the pages that follow the title page and/or in forewords and epilogues. *Innan Ganges flyter in i natten*, the poetry anthology quoted above, lists as many as 17 Swedish and Indian translators/collaborators. Other named contributors mentioned in this volume include the poets themselves, many of the intermediary translators and a great number of institutions, such as the original publishers, the publishers of the intermediary texts, the Swedish publisher (Tranan) and partner institutions that provided economic or other kinds of support, namely Sida, the Indian-Swedish book project, and the journal *Karavan*. In the series as a whole there were even more institutions involved, as not all the books in the series were published by Tranan.

In some of the forewords and epilogues, considerably more "contributors" are mentioned than those listed in the Appendix to this article. For instance, Katarina Sjöwall Trodden (2008), a translator of Basheer, gives her thanks to Basheer's friends and family members, including Basheer's youngest brother Abu, his niece Khadija, and his son and daughter Anees and Shahina. Furthermore, she mentions the contributions of M.N. Karassery, professor of Malayalam, the bookseller Sreetharan and the photographer Punaloor Rajan, among others. All in all, this makes up a very complex multiple translatorship.

It is noteworthy that the hierarchy between Swedish translators and Indian collaborators varies between the books. For *Flod* (River), featuring short stories by Ambai as translated by Birgitta Wallin, the title page indicates that "the Swedish translation is done from English translations and from the original Tamil texts (in collaboration with Sandhya Rao and Manorama Madhava Rao)" (Ambai 2008). In U.R. Anantha Murthy's [sic] (2001) *Samskara: Rit för en död man* [Samskara: A rite for a dead man], the Indian translator is named as a co-translator, not merely a collaborator. This is the only book of the series that does this, and interestingly it also includes separate epilogues by both the Swedish translator, Hans O. Sjöström, and the Indian, Vanamala Viswanatha. Viswanatha gets to speak in her own words, and her role is therefore highly visible. This makes it all the more interesting to note that A.K. Ramanujan, the translator of the English intermediary text on which the Swedish translation was based, is not mentioned on the title page, only in Sjöström's epilogue. The same goes for Basheer (2008) where the title page gives the original titles in Malayalam but neither the titles nor translators of the English collections in which they were published.

As a result, the translators of these published versions, who were highly instrumental in enabling the translation of these books into Swedish, unfairly come across as less important than the Indian collaborators. This is clear from the following example from Ambai (2008), whose title page provides the titles of the Tamil originals, the English translations and the translator into English, Lakshmi Holmström. Concerning her translation, Birgitta Wallin recalled that

> I spent a few weeks in Chennai, the capital of the state of Tamil Nadu, where Sandhya Rao, herself a translator, writer of children's books and publisher, and her mother, Manorama Madhva Rao, helped me to compare the English text I had used with Ambai's original in Tamil. We sat at Sandhya's dining table, where I could taste the nuances of the Tamil language together with some of the vegetarian dishes that appear in the book. Manorama was a wonderful chef. Sandhya's son would occasionally run to the grocer and come back with a spice (otherwise unknown to me) for me to smell. The best was when Sandhya's mother would sing some of the Tamil songs that are quoted here and there in the short stories. (2008, 157)

This shows how the Indian collaborator (and her mother) helped Wallin fill in some of the cultural knowledge gaps between the intermediate English translations that she worked from: what do the spices and food taste and smell like? What is behind the intertextual references to the songs? As important as this kind of information may have been to the translator, it should be noted that the published intermediary translation (and hence its translator) must have played a much more important role in the translation process than the Indian collaborator. The question then becomes why the collaborator is given so much more credit. One possible explanation could be the personal relationship between the two; another, which more directly targets the core of this article, would be that the existence of an Indian collaborator at least mitigates (rather than legitimizes) the breach of the directness norm.

In this regard it is also important to note that references to spices and foods recur throughout the paratexts of *Indiska biblioteket*, not only in forewords and epilogues but also in a few of the Swedish titles, such as *Kärlek, uppror och kardemummakärnor* [Love, revolt and cardamom seeds], which thus forefront the idea of exotic aromas. These references clearly make the foreign more foreign, in a way that resembles orientalism as first identified by Said (1978). It would be tempting to conclude that orientalism is all there is to it, but passages like Wallin's above may simultaneously reproduce stereotypes and make readers aware of the fact that there are many things in these texts that the translators have found difficult to represent in Swedish. In this sense, the passage above not only stereotypes the cultural representation, it also makes the translator's intervention visible.[6]

Another, though quite different example of how the collaboration worked and how the intervention is made visible can be found in the following lines from Viswanatha's epilogue to *Samskara*. Interestingly, this also refers to the use of one of the five senses – not smell or taste this time, but sound:

> To transmit the tone and atmosphere in a text is something that is incredibly difficult for a translator. It is more common to reconstruct the literary text word by word, line by line, or sentence by sentence. In this way it is possible to reconstruct the text literally, but what you often miss is the imagery and the tone of the text. What we did is that I marked the change of tone and checked that Hans had perceived it in the same way. If we agreed, I would read chosen excerpts aloud, first in Kannada and then in English, so that he could get an idea of the structure of the text. Assisted by our auditory imagination, we developed a feeling for the motion of the text, even though none of us could understand the language of the other. We managed to express the poetic, lyrical, satirical and descriptive tropes that Ananthamurthy employs so powerfully in his original in Kannada. Translating, which often means staring at cold print and turning it into yet more cold print, was turned into a warm and human experience, in which much more than the text was translated. May the tribe of collaborating translators grow! (Viswanatha 2001, 163–164; my back translation)

Viswanatha here draws attention to a very different kind of bridging from the cultural kind that Wallin identified above. Here, it is the text's aesthetics that these two translators try to convey, by means of sound and voice. It is worth noting that this aesthetic approach comes from an agent in the original culture, and that this is an unusual perspective on literature from the former European colonies in Scandinavian paratexts, which tend to be framed primarily as windows to these countries' reality and social conditions rather than marketed for their aesthetic values (see Alvstad 2012). The last lines of Viswanatha's epilogue are about the warm and human experience this collaboration entailed, echoing Wallin's portrayal of her stay in Chennai.

The way the translators worked with their Indian collaborators thus varied from one translation to another. One collaborator, Hena Basu, even produced her own translations of the texts as she considered that the best way to bridge the differences between the original and the published translations in English (Stolpe 2008, 293; Wallin 2008, 157).

The reception of *Indiska biblioteket* in the Swedish press

I have argued elsewhere (Alvstad 2012, 91) that an emphasis on geography, understood as cultural diversity and culture-specific learning, is one of two major Eurocentric strategic moves used by Swedish publishers when mediating literature from Africa, Asia and Latin America (the other being an emphasis on universalism). The analysis in the previous section makes clear that the agents involved in creating *Indiska biblioteket* inscribe themselves in this tradition as they stress cultural diversity and culture-specific learning and show little interest in discussing issues related to aesthetics.

Also in the reviews of the various installments of *Indiska biblioteket*, the general pattern is to write about the books as windows to Indian diversity rather than to discuss their aesthetic value. Peter Ortman (2002), in his review of the anthology of short stories published as *Kärlek, uppror och kardemummakärnor*, first lists some general traits about India and its many states, languages and religions, before summarizing that reading the anthology provides "a colorful, sensuous, entertaining, sometimes shocking, kaleidoscopic image of modern India". Here again we meet an account reminiscent of the orientalist discourse identified by Said (1978). Furthermore, the fictional accounts are taken as a direct representation of reality in a way that comes across as unreflective. Although literature undeniably can enhance cultural knowledge and understanding, the relation between the two cannot possibly be as transparent as presented here.

There are conspicuously many examples along the same orientalist line. I will here quote another review of the same book, as this reviewer so clearly manifests her awareness of how the reading deconstructs her prior conception of India. According to the reviewer,

> the truly great takeaway has been to stride into and get to know an unknown continent. For twenty-five years, ever since I was fifteen, I have longed to travel there. After reading *Kärlek, uppror och kardemummakärnor*, I realize that I haven't had a clue about what sort of country I longed to travel to. (Stig 2002)

Given this sudden recognition that her preconceived notions were off the mark, it is interesting that the reviewer seemingly allows this fictional account to help her construct a brand-new conception that, based as it is on solely one book, may be equally mistaken or limiting. There is no manifested awareness in this review, published under the title "En öppen dörr till okända världar" [An open door to unknown worlds], that fiction is a subjective, imagined representation of reality, and that the fictional world created by the author might actually have undergone many changes when translated, first into English and then into Swedish – and, even more precisely, translated into Swedish by translators who do not themselves have a thorough understanding of India, as they do not speak the languages of the originals they are translating. The fact that the short stories are translated via English is mentioned in passing, but also accepted precisely because of the door it opens:

> India is not a single world, but many. Over a hundred languages and thousands of dialects are spoken there. There are Hindus, Muslims and Sikhs, an intellectual middle class, Brahmins, and low-caste farmers fighting for a bundle of rice. In short, it is a huge country with a diversity that we in the West often choose to hide behind the image of a sacred cow. (Stig 2002)

The way the editors and translators argue for indirect translation seems to convince the reviewers, who do not question the indirectness of the translation but rather see the benefit of it opening up otherwise inaccessible literature. The idea of the capacity of literature to inform about reality and social conditions also passes uncritically to the reviewers, and in some instances even seems to be strengthened in the reviews as compared to the forewords and epilogues.[7] In sum, the target audience as represented by the reviewers seems not only to accept but also to appreciate stereotyped representations of a former colonized Other. Such readiness to read about Indian "reality" in this exotic packaging may be one of the most significant explanations for why they accept the violation of the directness norm.

In order to discover whether the indirect translations of the *Indiska biblioteket* series were more positively or negatively received than other indirect translations published about the same time, I conducted a new search in the Retriever database. The search string *via engelska* ("via English") yielded about 30 hits, referring to indirect translations.[8] The pattern seemed to be that it could be mentioned in reviews, but the fact that they were translated indirectly was seldom criticized, though neither was it celebrated. The few results with critical remarks referred to printed interviews with translators, such as Tobias Theander, a translator from Vietnamese; Per Erik Wahlund, a translator from Japanese; and, interestingly, also Meta Ottosson, one of the translators of *Indiska biblioteket*, who translated some of the poems that were originally written in English.

Concluding discussion

Indiska biblioteket provides considerable information about the collaborative translation process, and many kinds of collaborators are named. The Swedish translators are given paratextual space to write about their translation experience as well as their personal experiences in India. Many of the Swedish agents emphasize the striking differences between India and Sweden, but also how different Indian regions and social, linguistic and religious spheres are from one another. The few Indian collaborators who wrote paratexts of their own for the books stress both aesthetic factors and literary traditions to a higher degree than do the Swedish translators. The critical reception was strongly oriented towards cultural knowledge and understanding, and not so much the aesthetic values of the books, although there is some variation in this respect.

Indiska biblioteket offers something new to the Swedish target system, both in terms of literary works and how translational issues are addressed in the paratexts. It targets a wide audience rather than a scholarly one, as evidenced by paratexts explaining foreign words and cultural phenomena in a didactic way. The many journalists and reviewers who wrote about this series were almost unanimously positive. It is interesting that they as professional readers and commentators are so positive towards a series of indirect translations, when the related cultural policies are so averse to the practice. Even if these had been "common" direct translations, such a reception would have been surprising. It should be noted that what the cultural journalists and reviewers applaud is not the indirectness per se, but the very appearance of these books on the Swedish market. In other words, the opening up of translation policy seems to have played a major role in paving the way for this positive reception.

It is also worth noting that while stereotyped representations of an aromatic India are indeed part of how these books are presented, the reviews show an even greater willingness both to stereotype and to read the fictional accounts as direct representations of Indian reality. This readiness to consume and reproduce an orientalist discourse may also have played an important role in the series' success. A third explanation could be the fact that its installments overtly advocated the collaborative, indirect translation method employed.

Collaborations and explorations are part of how literature works, and we may wish also to let translation be part of that creative sphere. Some readers worry about what gets lost in translation, and presumably these are the same readers who worry about what gets lost in indirect translation. But would not the more relevant questions be: what is lost if we do not translate a given text at all? And what is lost when we are so restrictive about indirect translation? One answer, drawing heavily on what the editors and translators of *Indiska biblioteket* write about their practice, would be that if we do not translate indirectly, we clearly end up with many languages and literatures that never get translated. And if we translate from languages not usually translated into a certain language, we enrich the target literary system with new influences. Another answer, also inspired by the paratexts of *Indiska biblioteket*, is that literary texts enhance interpersonal understanding of, for example, other ways of thinking and being, and other living conditions and cultures. The relation between fiction and reality may not be as straightforward as some formulations by the collaborators and reviewers of *Indiska biblioteket* would suggest, but the alternatives – not to read literature, not to translate – would do more harm to interpersonal and intercultural understanding. I would therefore like to conclude this article with a call for more experimenting, more collaborations, more transgressive practices in literary and cultural exchange, as well as an equally strong call to the field of translation studies to explore such past, present and future practices.

Notes

1. Detailed information about titles, the original languages, source texts, intermediary texts, translators and other collaborators is presented in the Appendix.
2. The searches were conducted in the Retriever database using "Indiska biblioteket" and all the titles of the books as search strings.
3. "Det är naturligtvis principiellt sett önskvärt att litterär översättning inte sker via ett intermediärt språk."
4. Heilbron's (1999) distinction between central and peripheral comes from his analysis of the available data of translated books worldwide. According to Heilbron's analysis, English is by far the most central language: between 50% and 70% of all published translations in Europe in 1980 were translated from English, and Heilbron therefore describes its role as hypercentral. French, German and Russian each had a share of between 10% and 12% of the market in 1980 and are therefore considered to be central languages. Languages with 1–3% of the total proportion are considered to be semi-peripheral (for 1978 Heilbron lists Spanish, Italian, Danish, Swedish, Polish and Czech in this category). Among peripheral languages we find some languages with many speakers such as Chinese, Japanese, Arabic and Portuguese, and, as Heilbron (1999, 434) points out, this means that "the size of language groups is clearly not decisive for their degree of centrality in the translation system".
5. Although this is a Swedish book, the title page states in English that it was "first published in South Korea as *Omma rul Put'akhae*" and that it is "published by arrangement with Lennart Sane Agency" (Shin 2013, n.p.; quoted from the paperback edition).
6. On stereotypes in Scandinavian literary translations, see Refsdal (2016) and Senstad (2015).
7. One exception is Magnus Eriksson (2001), who emphasizes primarily aesthetic values in his review of Sobti's book. Eriksson argues that the novel is good, not because it was originally written in Hindi, but because it offers a synthesis of Hindu wisdom and Samuel Beckett.
8. Searches for *indirekt översättning* ("indirect translation"), *andrahandsöversättning* ("secondhand translation") and *intermediär översättning* ("intermediary translation") did not yield any interesting results, which suggests that these terms are not used in Swedish media.

Acknowledgement

I wish to thank Idun Heir Senstad and Signe Kårstad for their assistance.

Disclosure statement

No potential conflict of interest was reported by the author.

Funding

Research for this article was carried out under the auspices of the *Voices of Translation: Rewriting Literary Texts in a Scandinavian Context* project, which was supported by the Research Council of Norway (project no. 213246) and the Faculty of Humanities at the University of Oslo.

References

Alvstad, Cecilia. 2012. "The Strategic Moves of Paratexts: World Literature Through Swedish Eyes." *Translation Studies* 5 (1): 78–94.

Ambai. 2008. *Flod* [River]. Translated by Birgitta Wallin. Stockholm: Tranan.

Anantha Murthy, U. R. 2001. *Samskara: Rit för en död man* [Samskara: A Rite for a Dead Man]. Translated by Hans O. Sjöström, and Vanamala Viswanatha. Stockholm: Ordfront.

Arts Council Norway. 2016. "Retningslinjer for innkjøpsordningen for oversatt litteratur." [Guidelines for Support Purchase Grants for Translated Literature]. Accessed February 4, 2016, http://www.kulturradet.no/documents/10157/ac5d5ed2-91a8-43f5-aed7-c7ebb44b1162.

Basheer, Vaikom Muhammad. 2008. *Under mangoträdet* [Under the Mango Tree]. Translated by Katarina Sjöwall Trodden. Stockholm: Tranan.

Danish Arts Foundation. 2016. "Oversættelse og produktion" [Translation and Production]. Accessed February 4, 2016, http://www.kunst.dk/kunststoette/puljestamside/tilskud/oversaetterpuljen/.

Eriksson, Magnus. 2001. "Hinduisk visdom möter Beckett" [Hinduic Wisdom Meets Beckett]. *Svenska Dagbladet*, November 29. Accessed June 28, 2013, http://www.retriever-info.com/sv.

Grover, Teji. 2009. "På törstens berg: Om den samtida hindipoesin" [At The Mountain of Comfort: About Contemporary Hindi Poetry]. Translated by Birgitta Wallin. In Löfström, Thomas, and Birgitta Wallin. *Innan Ganges flyter in i natten* [Before Ganges Flows into the Night]. Translated by Lars Andersson, Jonas Ellerström, Lars Hermansson, Arne Johnsson, Ann Jäderlund, Marie Lundquist, Tomas Löfström, Niclas Nilsson, Meta Ottosson, Zac O'Yeah, Lasse Söderberg, and Birgitta Wallin. Stockholm: Tranan. 20–29.

Hasan, Anjum. 2009. "Att vattna öken: Om modern indisk-engelsk poesi" [To Water the Desert: About Anglo-Indian Poetry]. Translated by Arne Johnsson. In Löfström, Thomas, and Birgitta Wallin. *Innan Ganges flyter in i natten* [Before Ganges Flows into the Night]. Translated by Lars Andersson, Jonas Ellerström, Lars Hermansson, Arne Johnsson, Ann Jäderlund, Marie Lundquist, Tomas Löfström, Niclas Nilsson, Meta Ottosson, Zac O'Yeah, Lasse Söderberg, and Birgitta Wallin. Stockholm: Tranan. 220–230.

Heilbron, Johan. 1999. "Towards a Sociology of Translation Book Translations as a Cultural World-System." *European Journal of Social Theory* 2 (4): 429–444.

Hekkanen, Raila. 2014. "Direct Translation – Is It the Only Option? Indirect Translation of Finnish Prose Literature into English." In *True North: Literary Translation in the Nordic Countries*, edited by B. J. Epstein, 47–64. Newcastle upon Tyne: Cambridge Scholars Publishing.

Jansen, Hanne, and Anna Wegener. 2013. "Multiple Translatorship." In *Authorial and Editorial Voices in Translation, vol. 1 [Vita Traductiva 2]*, edited by Hanne Jansen, and Anna Wegener, 1–39. Montreal: Éditions québécoises de l'œuvre.

Löfström, Thomas, and Birgitta Wallin. 2008. "Förord" [Preface]. In Basheer, Vaikom Muhammad, *Under mangoträdet* [Under the Mango Tree]. Translated by Katarina Sjöwall Trodden. Stockholm: Tranan. 7.

Löfström, Thomas, and Birgitta Wallin. 2009a. *Innan Ganges flyter in i natten* [Before Ganges Flows into the Night]. Translated by Lars Andersson, Jonas Ellerström, Lars Hermansson, Arne Johnsson, Ann Jäderlund, Marie Lundquist, Tomas Löfström, Niclas Nilsson, Meta Ottosson, Zac O'Yeah, Lasse Söderberg, and Birgitta Wallin. Stockholm: Tranan.

Löfström, Thomas, and Birgitta Wallin. 2009b. "Översättare på ordens strand" [Translators on the Shore of Words]. In Löfström, Thomas, and Birgitta Wallin. *Innan Ganges flyter in i natten* [Before Ganges Flows into the Night]. Translated by Lars Andersson, Jonas Ellerström, Lars Hermansson, Arne Johnsson, Ann Jäderlund, Marie Lundquist, Tomas Löfström, Niclas Nilsson, Meta Ottosson, Zac O'Yeah, Lasse Söderberg, and Birgitta Wallin. Stockholm: Tranan. 11–18.

Marin-Lacarta, Maialen. 2012. "A Brief History of Translations of Modern and Contemporary Chinese Literature in Spain (1949–2009)." *1611: Revista de historia de la traducción / A Journal of Translation History/ Revista D'història de la traducció* 6: 1–7. Accessed February 4, 2016, http://www.traduccionliteraria.org/1611/art/marin2.htm.

Norsk oversetterforening. 2016. "Flerstemt, litterært oversetterkurs" [Multivoiced, literary Translation Course]. Accessed August 30, 2016, http://oversetterforeningen.no/flerstemt-litteraert-oversetterkurs-3/.

Ortman, Peter. 2002. "Review of *Kärlek, uppror och kardemummakärnor*" [Review of Love, Revolt and Cardamom Seeds]. *Helsingborgs Dagblad*, February 20. Accessed June 28, 2013, http://www.retriever-info.com/sv.

Översättarcentrum. 2016. "Sök översättare, översätter från" [Search Translators Translating From]. Accessed August 30, 2016, http://www.oversattarcentrum.se/sv.html/om-oss.

Refsdal, Eva. 2016. "When a 'Girl' Becomes 'An Attractive Little Number': Stereotyped Representations of Latin America in Literary Translation and Reception in 1960s Norway." PhD diss., University of Oslo.

Said, Edward, W. 1978. *Orientalism*. New York: Pantheon Books.

Satchidanandan, K. 2009. *Från revolutionär kamp till litterär mångfald* [From Revolutionary Struggle to Literary Manifoldness]. Translated by Tomas Löfström. In Löfström, Thomas, and Birgitta Wallin. *Innan Ganges flyter in i natten* [Before Ganges Flows into the Night]. Translated by Lars Andersson, Jonas Ellerström, Lars Hermansson, Arne Johnsson, Ann Jäderlund, Marie Lundquist, Tomas Löfström, Niclas Nilsson, Meta Ottosson, Zac O'Yeah, Lasse Söderberg, and Birgitta Wallin. Stockholm: Tranan. 142–151.

Senstad, Idun Heir. 2015. "Bokomslag som formidling: Cubanske romaner i norsk innpakning" [Book Covers as Mediation: Cuban Novels in Norwegian Packaging]. In *Litteratur- og kulturformidling: Nye analyser og perspektiver* [Mediation of Literature and Culture: New Analyses and Perspectives], edited by Helge Ridderstrøm and Tonje Vold, 166–188. Oslo: Pax.

Shin, Kyung-Sook. 2013. *Ta hand om sin mor* [Looking after One 's Mom]. Translated by Molle Kanmert Sjölander. Stockholm: Norstedt. (Paperback edition. The Swedish hardcover was published in 2012, but I have not been able to consult the title page of that edition).

Sida. 2016. "About Us: Our Mission." Accessed February 4, 2016, http://www.sida.se/English/About-us/Our-mission/.

Sjöström, Hans O. 2001. "Experimentet" [The Experiment]. In Anantha Murthy, U. R. *Samskara: Rit för en död man* [Samskara: A Rite for a Dead Man]. Translated by Hans O. Sjöström, and Vanamala Viswanatha. Stockholm: Ordfront. 161–162.

Sjöwall Trodden, Katarina. 2008. "Efterord" [Afterword]. In Basheer, Vaikom Muhammad, Under mangoträdet [Under the Mango Tree]. Translated by Katarina Sjöwall Trodden. Stockholm: Tranan. 211–219.

Stig, Oline. 2002. "En öppen dörr till okända världar" [A Door to Unknown Worlds]. *Sydsvenskan*, 5 January 2002. Accessed July 2 2013, http://www.retriever-info.com/sv.

Stillinger, Jack. 1991. *Multiple Authorship and the Myth of the Solitary Genius*. New York: Oxford University Press.

Stolpe, Jan. 2008. "Översättarens efterord" [The Translator's Afterword]. In Devi, Mahasweta. *Branden i hjärtat: Berättelser från Bengalen* [The Fire in the Heart: Stories from Bengal]. Translated by Jan Stolpe. Stockholm: Ordfront. 293.

Swedish Arts Council. 2016a. "Support Scheme for Swedish Literature in Translation." Accessed February 4, 2016, http://www.kulturradet.se/sv/swedishliterature/Grants/Translation-Grants1/.

Swedish Arts Council. 2016b. "Utgångspunkter för bedömning av litteraturstödet" [Points of Departure for the Evaluation of the Support Scheme for Literature]. Accessed February 4, 2016, http://www.kulturradet.se/sv/bidrag/litteratur/Litteraturstod/Bedomning-av-litteraturstod/.

Tegelberg, Elisabeth. 2011. "Nyöversättning: När, hur och varför?" [Retranslation: When, How and Why?]. *TfL* 2011 (3–4): 77–90.

Toury, Gideon. 1995/2012. *Descriptive Translation Studies and Beyond*. 2nd rev ed. Amsterdam: John Benjamins.

Viswanatha, Vanamala. 2001. "Experimentet" [The Experiment]. Translated by Hans O. Sjöström. In Anantha Murthy, U. R. *Samskara: Rit för en död man* [Samskara: A Rite for a Dead Man]. Translated by Hans O. Sjöström, and Vanamala Viswanatha. Stockholm: Ordfront. 162–164.

Wallin, Birgitta. 2008. "Efterord" [Afterword]. In Ambai. *Flod* [River]. Translated by Birgitta Wallin. Stockholm: Tranan. 153–157.

Appendix: The 11 books of the series *Indiska biblioteket* by date of appearance

1. *Samskara: Rit för en död man*.
  Anantha Murthy, U.R. 2001. *Samskara: Rit för en död man* [Samskara: A rite for a dead man]. Translated by Hans O. Sjöström and Vanamala Viswanatha. Stockholm: Ordfront.
  Original title: *Samskara*.
  Language of the original: Kannada.
  Intermediary language: English. Translation into English by A.K. Ramanujan.
  The Swedish edition includes two epilogues, and an explanatory list of words and terms.

2. *Lyssna min dotter*.
  Sobti, Krishna. 2001. *Lyssna min dotter* [Listen, my daughter]. Translated by Annika Persson. Stockholm: Tranan.
  Original title: *Ai Ladki*.
  Language of the original: Hindi.
  Intermediary language: English.
  The Swedish edition includes an epilogue by the translator. She read a couple of very different English translations by Shivnath, and Anjali Singh and Tarun Bhartiya and explains that she went through the text in collaboration with Chandra Ramakrishnan at Katha editorial house. She consulted the author, and discussed particular problems with Sukrita Kemar and Shivnath.

3. *Kärlek, uppror och kardemummakärnor: Berättelser från Indien*.
  Wallin, Birgitta, and Tomas Löfström, eds. 2001. *Kärlek, uppror och kardemummakärnor: Berättelser från Indien* [Love, revolt and cardamom seeds: Stories from India]. Translated by Birgitta Wallin, Tomas Löfström, Roy Isaksson, Örjan Sjögren, Meta Ottosson, Marianne Eyre, Marianne Öjerskog, Hanna Axén, Boel Unnerstad, Jimmy Hofsö and Hans O. Sjöström. Stockholm: Tranan.
  Languages of the original: Hindi, Urdu, Bengali, Marathi, Odia, Tamil, Kannada, Malayalam, Assamese and English.
  Intermediary language: English.
  The anthology includes a foreword by the editors and an explanatory list of words and terms, and a biographical presentation of the authors.

4. *Dagar i Mahuldiha: Berättelser & reportage från östra Indien*.
  Agnihotri, Anita. 2006. *Dagar i Mahuldiha: Berättelser & reportage från östra Indien* [Days in Mahuldiha: Stories & reports from Eastern India]. Translated by Joar Tiberg. Stockholm: Tranan.
  No Indian collaborator mentioned.
  Language of the original: Bengali.

Intermediary language: English.

The texts were selected from the following collection: Barhan, Kalpana, ed. 2001. *Forest Interludes: A Collection of Journals and Fiction*. Translated by Kalpana Bardhan. New Dehli: Kali for Women. (Kali for Women is now Zubaan, www.zubaanbooks.com.)

The Swedish edition includes an epilogue by the editors and an explanatory list of words and terms.

5. *Berättelsen på min rygg: Indiens daliter i uppror mot kastsystemet. Prosa, essäer, dokument.*

Hardtmann, Eva-Maria, and Vimal Thorat (in collaboration with Tomas Löfstöm and Birgitta Wallin), eds. 2006. *Berättelsen på min rygg: Indiens daliter i uppror mot kastsystemet. Berättelser, essäer, dokument* [The story on my back: The Dalits of India in rebellion against the caste system. Prose, essays, documents]. Translated by Ann Björkhem, Hans O. Sjöström and Zac O'Yeah. Stockholm: Ordfront.

Languages of the original: English, Hindi, Kannada, Marathi and Tamil.

Intermediary language: English.

One short story was translated directly from Kannada by Vishwanatha and Sjöström. The essays and documents were in most cases translated from English originals.

The book includes a foreword by the editors of *Indiska biblioteket*. The translator Vanamala Vishwanatha's collaboration is mentioned only in the editor's foreword, not on the title page. The book also includes an introductory text to the Dalits and the caste system, by editors Hardtmann and Thorat, and an explanatory list of words and terms, biographical notes on the authors, and a bibliography.

6. *Detta land som aldrig var vår moder: Dikter av indiska dalitpoeter och bilder av Savi Sawarkar.*

Hardtmann, Eva-Marie, and Vimal Thorat (in collaboration with Tomas Löfström and Birgitta Wallin), eds. 2006. *Detta land som aldrig var vår moder: Dikter av indiska dalitpoeter och bilder av Savi Sawarkar* [This country that was never our mother: Poems by Indian Dalit poets]. Translated by Lars Andersson, Tomas Löfström and Birgitta Wallin. Stockholm: Tranan.

Languages of the originals: Marathi and Tamil.

Intermediary language: English.

Translations from the original language into English by Priya Adarkar, Vilas Sarang, Charudatta Bhagwat, Jayant Karve, Eleanor Zelliott, Dilip Chitre, Shanta Gokhale, Asha Mundlay, Laurie Hovell, V.G. Nand, Nissim Ezekiel, Philip Engblom, S. K. Thorat, Anushiya Sivanarayanan, Sylvie Martinez and Vimal Thorat.

Collaborating translators: A.K. Ramanujan, Pam Espeland.

The Swedish edition includes a foreword by the editors, an introduction by the translators and explanatory notes.

The poems were selected from:

Dangle, Arjun, ed. 1992. *Poisoned Bread: Translations from Modern Marathi Dalit Literature*. Bombay: Orient Longman.

Anand, Mulk Raj, and Eleanor Zelliot, eds. 1992. *An Anthology of Dalit Litterature*. New Dehli: Gyan Publishing House.

7. *Branden i hjärtat: Berättelser från Bengalen.*

Devi, Mahasweta. 2008. *Branden i hjärtat: Berättelser från Bengalen* [The fire in the heart: Stories from Bengal]. Translated by Jan Stolpe. Stockholm: Ordfront.

The story "Jakten" was translated by Birgitta Wallin.

Indian collaborator: Hena Basu, as named in Jan Stolpe's afterword (p. 293).

Language of the original: Bengali.

Intermediary language: English.

The texts were selected from European published translations (44 translations in English, 10 in German and 4 in French are listed in the bibliography at the end of the book).

The publication includes a foreword by Wallin, an epilogue by Stolpe, nine pages of explanatory notes, an explanatory list of words and terms, and an extensive bibliography of translations into English, German and French.

8. *Den heliga papegojan och andra historier om Akbar och Birbal.*

Stinus, Sara Mathai, reteller. 2008. *Den heliga papegojan och andra historier om Akbar och Birbal* [The holy parrot and other stories about Akbar and Birbal]. Translated by Marie Norin and Catharina Andersson. Stockholm: Karavan.

Language of the original and intermediary text: it is translated from Danish into Swedish. Mathai Stinus heard the stories in Kannada as a child.

The Swedish edition includes a foreword by Wallin, and an introduction by Mathai Stinus. These explain that the stories about Akbar and Birbal date several centuries back, and that Mathai Stinus, who is originally from Kerala but has lived most of her life in Denmark, first heard these stories from her father, and later read them in different versions in books.

9. *Flod.*

Ambai. 2008. *Flod* [River]. Translated by Birgitta Wallin. Stockholm: Tranan.

Language of the original: Tamil.

Intermediary language: English.

The Swedish edition includes an epilogue by the translator and an explanatory list of words and terms, and explanatory notes.

The Swedish translations were done from the English translations by Lakshmi Holmström, published in the collections *A Purple Sea* (1997) and *In a Forest, a Deer* (2006), and from the original Tamil texts (in collaboration with Sandhya Rao and Manorama Madhava Rao). The short stories were originally selected from three different collections in Tamil: *Siragugal Muriyum* (1976), *Veettin Moolaiyil Oru Samayalarai* (1988) and *Kaatil Oru Maan* (2000).

10. *Innan Ganges flyter in i natten.*

Löfström, Thomas, and Birgitta Wallin, eds. 2009. *Innan Ganges flyter in i natten* [Before Ganges flows into the night]. Translated by Lars Andersson, Jonas Ellerström, Lars Hermansson, Arne Johnsson, Ann Jäderlund, Marie Lundquist, Tomas Löfström, Niclas Nilsson, Meta Ottosson, Zac O'Yeah, Lasse Söderberg and Birgitta Wallin. Stockholm: Tranan.

Languages of the original poems: Hindi, Malayalam, English.

Intermediary language: English.

The translations were done in collaboration with Teji Grover, Anjum Hasan, Jyotsna Milan, Rizio Raj Yohannan and K. Satchidanandan.

The anthology includes a general preface with background information; individual prefaces, written by the Indian collaborators (Grover, Satchidanandan and Hasan), preceding each section; an explanatory list of words, terms, personal names and places; commentaries on some poems; biographical notes on poets and translators; list of previous publications in Swedish; and list of sources where the poems were originally published.

11. *Under mangoträdet: Tre berättelser.*

Basheer, Vaikom Muhammad. 2008. *Under mangoträdet* [Under the mango tree]. Translated by Katarina Sjöwall Trodden. Stockholm: Tranan.

Original titles: "Baalyakalasakhi", 1944; "Entuppuppaykkoraanendaarnnu", 1951; and "Pathummade Aadu", 1959.

Language of the original: Malayalam.

Translated from Malayalam in collaboration with Rizio Raj Yohannan.

Intermediary languages: English and French. English translation by R.E. Asher and Achamma Coilparampil Chandersekaran, 1980. The story "Morfar hade en elefant!" [Grandfather had an elephant!] was translated via the French translation by Dominique Vitalyo, 2005. Vitalyo translated directly from Malayalam.

The Swedish edition includes a preface by the editors of the series and an epilogue by the translator. It also includes an explanatory list of words and terms.

Institutionalized intermediates: Conceptualizing Soviet practices of indirect literary translation

Susanna Witt

ABSTRACT

In the Soviet Union, practices of indirect literary translation, particularly the use of interlinear intermediates, were institutionalized in the early 1930s through special terminology, specific administrative treatment within the literary apparatus, and educational efforts. Such practices continued until the end of the Soviet era, but were intensely debated and criticized, rendering problems of indirect translation both visible and articulated in a unique way. Drawing on archival sources, this article presents an overview of such issues, taking into consideration the heretofore scant attention given the subject in both Western and Russian scholarship. Conceptualizing the massive Soviet experience in the field, it aims at providing new perspectives on the phenomenon of indirect translation.

Introduction

Although indirect translation has been – and still is – practised widely in situations of intercultural exchange around the world, there is one context that stands out because of the systematic way in which intermediate texts were used as a translational tool for a period of more than 60 years. I have in mind the Soviet Union, where such practices were an indispensable part of the large-scale translation project involved in the creation of a Soviet literature. The institutional and planned character of these activities, as well as the large volume of texts processed in this way until the end of the Soviet era, distinguish the period from earlier epochs in Russian cultural history, even if indirect translation has always played a significant role, especially in the earlier stages (Zaborov 1963; Zaborov 2011). During the eighteenth century, English literature reached Russian readers via French and German intermediates. French was the most prominent of the mediating languages until the mid-nineteenth century, rendering, for example, Madame de Staël the most important agent in "acquainting the reading Russia with the works of the great German poets" (Zaborov 1963, 71). Toward the end of the nineteenth century, indirect translation from Western languages became rare, although smaller literatures such as Dutch and Scandinavian were still often translated from German editions.

Indirect translation in pre-revolutionary Russia was thus largely a matter of "relay translation" as defined by Dollerup (2000) – that is, when the mediating text is a work in its own right with its own target audience. It also corresponds in an uncomplicated way to the standard definition of indirect translation provided by Kittel and Frank, involving three different langugages: "any translation based on a source (or sources) which is itself a translation into a language other than the language of the original or the target language" (1991, 3). Three languages were involved when Calderón was translated into Russian via German in the 1820s, or Walter Scott from French (which was the rule up to the 1830s) (Zaborov 1963, 67, 70). Similar examples may be cited from Soviet times as well, the mediating language generally being Russian – a fact reflecting the status of this language as a lingua franca of the Union. These cases were principally of three types. First, works of world literature would typically be translated into the many languages of the Union via Russian translations, as when Shakespeare, Defoe, Dickens and Schiller were translated into Georgian from Russian editions (Zaborov 2011, 2071). Second, the "literatures of the peoples of the USSR" (an administrative-bureaucratic category comprising all the "non-Russian" literatures) were, almost without exception, translated into other European languages via Russian editions. Examples include the Armenian Vakhtang Ananian, who was translated into Czech, Polish and English from Russian (Zaborov 2011, 2071). Third, and finally, "literatures of the peoples of the USSR" were frequently translated into the languages of the other peoples of the Union from Russian versions (Witt 2013b, 165).

Only a minority of the indirect literary translations produced in the Soviet Union, however, were of a kind that falls neatly into conventional categories. The most widespread indirect practice was instead the use of intermediate interlinears, so-called *podstrochniki* (something located under the line). Here, the crude intermediate (the *podstrochnik*) was in the same language as the target text, rendering the entire transfer operation a translational hybrid involving an interlingual as well as an intralingual step (Jakobson 1959, 233). Typically, the two steps were carried out separately with no contact occurring between the respective agents. This was partly due to the significant geographical distance between centre and periphery in the Union: the *podstrochnik* was often produced locally in a Union republic and forwarded to a final translator based in Moscow or Leningrad. In this way, for example, the Dagestani bard Suleiman Stal'skii was translated in the 1930s by poets Nikolai Ushakov and Semen Lipkin, who received their intermediates "through a number of instances",[1] thus precluding communication with the producer of the *podstrochnik* and the author (or alleged author) of the ultimate source text. This feature distinguishes the Soviet case from most related practices that can be found elsewhere; for example, collaborations between (monolingual) poets and native speakers resulting in joint translations which are not uncommon in the anglophone world. It is, therefore, this particular practice and the problems related to it that are in focus for the present article, which builds on and develops my earlier research on the phenomenon, viewed as "a shorthand of empire" (Witt 2013a, 159).[2]

Part and parcel of the official system of Soviet literature, the *podstrochnik* in fact enabled this very literature to emerge as a multinational entity. In view of the large number of languages spoken within the USSR – approximately 150 at the end of the Soviet period (Grenoble 2003, 2) – and the lack of corresponding linguistic competence among translators, intermediate interlinears were accepted as a necessary aid in translations from the "nationalities languages" into Russian and also between these languages themselves (frequently with the use of a Russian interlinear). They were common in translation of literatures from outside the USSR as well, from not only distant languages such as Chinese, Korean and Japanese, but also European ones such as Hungarian, Finnish and even some Slavic languages. The method was used by well-known and lesser-known translators alike. Among the famous authors who practised it were Boris Pasternak (cf. Witt 2015), Anna Akhmatova, Nikolai Zabolotskii and Marina Tsvetaeva.

Since (in)directness of translation is a parameter not often reflected in bibliographies (a general problem, cf. Ringmar 2007, 7f.), indirect evidence has to be sought in order to calculate the extension of the phenomenon. We know, for example, that in 1956, 67% of all fiction literature issued in the USSR consisted of translations (Pechat' SSSR, 88) and that nearly half of this originated within the Union, an "overwhelming majority" of which was produced with the help of intermediate interlinears (Antokol'skii, Auezov, and Ryl'skii 1955, 12). At approximately the same time, in 1958, the Soviet Union was awarded a gold medal at the World Exhibition in Brussels as the country with the greatest number of published translations (Bagno and Kazanskii 2011, 2088).

In the Soviet-Russian context, intralingual (final) translators relying on interlinears came to be regarded – and to regard themselves – unequivocally as translators. These circumstances, arguably, contributed to the obscurity of the practice, which also involved near-total anonymity for the producers of the interlingual translation, the so-called *podstrochnikisty*. There is, however, one valuable source of information available; namely, documentation originating from within the Soviet literary apparatus. Although the use of intermediate interlinears was accepted and tolerated as a "temporary solution", it was intensely debated and criticized throughout the Soviet period. Problems of indirect translation were thereby articulated and made explicit in a unique way. Drawing on such archival material, this article provides an overview of issues figuring in the administrative treatment of *podstrochnik* translation and examines the ways the practice was conceptualized by the various agents of translation (Milton and Bandia 2009) at the time.

If practices of indirect translation generally have drawn relatively little scholarly attention, this is especially true for translation carried out with the help of interlinears. Evaluating entries dealing with indirect translation in the de Gruyter *Encyclopedia of Translation Studies*, Birgit Schultze notes that "interlinear translation, notwithstanding its frequency and geographical extensions, is largely ignored in the entries" (2014, 517). In the Russian context, Mikhail Gasparov remarked that

> we have talked and written a lot about the interlinear, but we have studied it little …. [T]ranslations from interlinears have been done and are still carried out in enormous quantities but there are almost no theoretical observations as to the practice. (2001, 361)

In one of the few articles on the topic, Galina Vanechkova argues that

> the work of the mediator preparing an interlinear – an extremely important and honorable labor – should enter the discipline of translation studies and find its place in studies dealing with the transfer of an original work into another cultural and linguistic milieu from the point of view of communication theory, comparative literature, psychology, sociology, and language. (1978, 11)

In the following, focus will be largely on the sociology of *podstrochnik* translation, involving the institutions, procedures and individual agents concerned. Particular attention will be devoted to issues of control and education on the part of the Soviet literary apparatus as reflected in the archival documentation, as well as to the various types of translational agency made possible through the practice. As will be seen, throughout the material the ontological and epistemological problems actualized by this specific form of indirect translation surface. By bringing in the voices of individual agents, I also hope to contribute to the historical visibility of translators.

Institutional framework

Literary translation in the Soviet Union was part of a larger project of culture planning (Even Zohar 2008) on several levels: the creation of "Soviet literature" as a canon of representative expressions of nationalities cultures and selected works of world literature, and the creation of nationalities cultures as indigenous canons involving translations from Russian as well as world literature (Witt 2011). Thus, translation was also part of Soviet nationalities policies, a fact reflected in the institutional infrastructure of Soviet literature. Within the Union of Soviet Writers (established in 1934), translational issues were managed at both the Translators' Section and the Nationalities Commission.[3] Another institution involved in the production and control of intermediate interlinears was the Soviet Academy of Sciences, which conducted such work at the level of its local branches, especially in the republics of Central Asia.

A virtual boom of translation from nationalities literature took place in the second half of the 1930s, following Maksim Gorky's speech at the First Congress of Soviet Writers in August 1934, where he emphasized the need for such translations in the process of "organizing the all-union literature as a whole" (*Pervyi s"ezd, 680*).[4] Gorky also initiated a periodical anthology to showcase the literature of the various republics in Russian translation. Later turned into a journal, this publication, *Druzhba narodov* (Peoples' friendship) was an important outlet for translations mediated by interlinears. It was issued by the State Publishing House for Literature (GIKhL, later Khudozhestvennaia literatura) which included a department for the "literatures of the peoples of the USSR" with a significant output of books by nationalities authors in Russian translation. In addition, the newspapers of the time frequently carried translated "non-Russian" literary material, also produced mainly with the help of interlinears. The production was intimately linked to the dynamics of literary politics as expressed, for example, in the many jubilees of various authors and symbolically important works that were to place them firmly in the canon of Soviet culture. In 1940–41, for example, there were jubilees in connection with the following occasions: the 800th anniversary of the Kalmuck epos *Dzhangar*, the 500th birthday of the Uzbek (Chagatay) author Navoi, the 800th birthday of the Azerbaijani (in fact, Persian) poet Nizami, the 100th birthday of the Georgian writer Tsereteli, the 50th birthday of the Chuvash author Ivanov, the 75th anniversary of the death of Ukrainian author Franko and the 75th birthday of his compatriot Kotsiubyn'skyi, and the 80th birthday of the Kirgiz writer Satylganov, as well as jubilees for the Turkmen folk poet Kimine, the Kirgiz Takhtabul and the Dagestani Tsadasa – all involving organizational efforts, including translation issues, on the part of the Union of Soviet Writers.[5] Another factor prompting the need for such translations (generally produced from interlinears) were the festivals featuring various nationalities cultures (*dekady*) which were held regularly in Moscow and Leningrad in the 1930s and 1940s (Witt 2011, 164f.).

A central phenomenon when it comes to translation from intermeditate interlinears in the USSR were the bards – representatives of oral folk traditions mainly in Central Asia and the Caucasus – who were appropriated by the Soviet literary apparatus for propaganda purposes. The most well-known of these figures, the Kazakh folk poet Dzhambul, has been cited by Gideon Toury (2005) as an instance of pseudotranslation.[6] Toury's claim that "nobody has ever encountered that man's poems in praise of the regime in anything but Russian" (ibid., 14) is, however, inaccurate, if only because there exist a number of Dzhambul editions in the Kazakh language (Witt 2011, 160). In actual fact, the term "pseudotranslation" does not quite apply to cases such as Dzhambul or the equally famous Dagestani (Lezgian) bard Suleiman Stal'skii. As evidenced in the archival material, these cases (and other similar ones) featured a complex set of transfer operations, including the use of interlinear intemediates, which resulted in a series of texts with various ontological status. After the appearance of Dzhambul (then aged 90) on the literary stage in 1936, an institutional framework was set up to facilitate his activities: a secretariat, a service apparatus and a bureau of interlinear translators.[7] The (supposedly) illiterate bard was assigned personal secretaries, well-known Kazakh poets, who were to write down what he composed or performed on topical political themes as well as material from his earlier pre-revolutionary production (purportedly reaching back to the 1880s). From these texts, interlinear translations were made into Russian, either by the Kazakh poets themselves or by others, after which an intralingual translation was produced by a Russian translator (a "poet-translator", as this category was designated). A better term than pseudotranslation would perhaps be "constellational production", since this was a process involving several agents, often in fixed constellations consisting of a native agent of transcription, an interlinear translator and a final Russian translator. The end product, in turn, often became a source text for further translations into other nationalities languages, and, after World War II, into the languages of countries belonging to the Eastern Bloc. This was, of course, the case only for the most famous of the bards, such as Dzhambul and Stal'skii. The emergence of this kind of literature produced a significant corpus of translational lore, anecdotal conversation pieces with a broad circulation in intelligentsia discourse during Soviet times. The details of such practices and their actual extent are, however, possible to reconstruct through archival material.

Although the bardic literature was an extreme example of complex mediation in the Soviet literary system, many of its constitutive features were part of indirect practices in other contexts of nationalities translation. As I have argued elsewhere (Witt 2013a, 160), the authenticity of the various texts produced (which, obviously, may legitimately be questioned in many cases) is of lesser relevance from the point of view of translation scholarship; the main interest here is represented by the varying conceptions of translation and translation practices that are revealed as the literary apparatus tried to manage and control the production.

The interlinear intermediate and agents of interlinear translation

The ontological and epistemological problems related to the use of interlinear translation have been touched upon by Galina Vanechkova (1978), cited above. Assuming that a case of direct translation may be represented by the simplified scheme O – I –T (original – interpretation – translation), Vanechkova visualizes interlinear translation as O – I – IL – I –T (original, interpretation, interlinear, interpretation, translation). However, this scheme, she argues, does not express the complexity of the change that occurs. Here, the "process of apperception [*appertseptsiia*]", involving somebody else's experience, which may explain a differing interpretation and various translational displacements, gets significantly more complicated as it proceeds through a mediator:

> If we take into account the claim made by scholars of aesthetics that a work of art becomes an artifact at the moment of its perception [*vospriiatie*], and that an active interrelationship between author and reader is indispensable for the artifact to come into being and to have an influence on the subject (in our case the translator), it becomes clear that this moment will be deformed if a prose version is used to render a work of poetry. In this case the work is an artifact for the author of the interlinear while the [final] translator is dealing with a semifinished product that is a work of a totally different quality. The latter is expected to turn this auxiliary translation back into an original, to create an integrated work of art capable of realizing itself as an artifact. (Ibid., 12)

Vanechkova's understanding of the aesthetic process and the realization of the "artifact" in relation to interlinear translation (apparently informed by Prague structuralists Jan Mukařovský and Felix Vodička, although they are not explicitly invoked) leads her to a principal denial of the possibilities of such translation. Since the aesthetic potential of the ultimate source text resides in its "particular correlation (or lack of correlation) between rhythm, rhyme, images, content", the final translator finds him/herself deprived of the "emotional influence" that affects the first translator – the most important factor for "the emergence of a high quality translation" (1978, 13). However, Vanechkova remarks, such a complex mediation is of significant theoretical interest. Therefore, "it is indispensable that the *podstrochnik* be accessible to scholars studying the translation process and translation as such" (ibid., 12).

Expressing a source-oriented ethos, Vanechkova's analysis may productively be related to Gideon Toury's discussion of "the two senses of 'literary translation' " (1995, 168). Toury makes a distinction between "the translation of literary texts" and "literary translation", respectively, where the former is "the translation of texts which are regarded as literary in the *source* culture … where the focus is on the retention (or better still, reconstruction) of the source text's internal web of relationships", while the latter is "the translation of a text … in such a way that the product can be acceptable as literary to the recipient culture" (ibid., 168). Thus, none of the steps in the complex act of translation carried out with the help of an intermediate interlinear can be designated "a translation of a literary text" in Toury's sense. The making of the *podstrochnik* from the ultimate source text would at best constitute a "linguistically-motivated translation", "yielding a product which is well-formed in terms of the target syntax, grammar and lexicon, even if it does not fully conform to any target model of text formation" (ibid., 171).[8] The final step of the operation constitutes almost by definition a "literary translation", involving "the imposition of conformity conditions … to models and norms which are deemed literary at the target end" (ibid., 171). This aspect is emphasized in the Russian standard designation of the agents of this final step as *poety-perevodchiki*, poet-translators.

Vanechkova, a Russian scholar who left the Soviet Union in 1954 and pursued a career at Charles University in Prague, does not comment on the practice in relation to the Soviet experience, but her sharp rejection of it is arguably polemical. Her only (implicit) reference to the USSR is a critique of inaccuracies in Konstantin Simonov's translation of a poem by the Czech modernist Vítěslav Nezval, made from an anonymous interlinear (Vanechkova 1978, 12). The practice arguably became a signature of Soviet power, drawing attention to its colonialist aspects (cf. Witt 2013a, 179).

In the Soviet treatment of *podstrochnik* translation, attitudes fluctuated over time, but total rejection was never an option. Various aspects of the problems pinpointed by Vanechkova surfaced regularly within the institutions mentioned above and were articulated largely in terms of professionalization and politics. The first serious discussions of the *podstrochnik* practice took place within the translators' corporation in 1933 as an issue related to the professionalization of the "cadres" in view of the imminent inclusion of their organization into the Union of Soviet Writers, which was to replace all previous literary organizations in 1934 (Witt 2013b; Zemskova 2013).

Documentation concerning the registration and assessment of translators at this stage reveals an unwillingness to characterize even the people working with the help of interlinears as translators. A 1934 report states that "their work can not be called translational and they need the appropriate education".[9] Educational efforts were called for also in connection with the producers of the interlinears, the *podstrochnikisty*. They made up a specific administrative category within the Translators' Section, the working plan for which in 1934 foresees registration of these persons and assessment of their knowledge of Russian as well as "a series of lectures about the technique of making interlinear intermediates", and the "issuing of an instruction on how to make the interlinear intermediate".[10] Howerver, the low level of education on the part of these agents as well as their "randomness" were lasting concerns within the literary apparatus.

The changing attitude toward the use of interlinear intermediates may be illustrated by the administrative treatment of the case of author-turned-translator Ezra Levontin.[11] His application for membership of the Union of Soviet Writers was turned down in 1935 on the grounds that "literary processing [*oformlenie*] of an interlinear cannot be regarded a translation".[12] In 1938, however, Levontin's candidature was approved, along with that of other translators working mainly with the help of interlinears.[13] This time was the peak of "nationalities translation" in the USSR. Although there had been hopes that language courses would eliminate the need for intermediates, the results to this end were meagre, and efforts were eventually concentrated mainly on improving and controlling the intermediate practices.[14] Within the Translators' Section criticism was occasionally voiced – "Comrades, of course there are moments when we fall short, but let us not make a norm or working principle out of it"[15] – but there were obvious grounds for playing down the significance of language competence in view of widening professional (and material) perspectives. As argued at the same meeting (in 1934) by the poet Osip Kolychev, who became one of the translators of the Dagestani bard Suleiman Stal'skii,

> [h]ow often isn't it that a comrade has excellent command of the [ultimate source] language, but the translation is such that you want to cry. It's better that he doesn't know any language at all, but is able to give us real poetry. It is not enough to know a language, you have to possess the specific talent of a translator, that is, you have to discern the talent of the other, a higher poetical judgment. ... I think that the term translation has become antiquated.[16]

The ontological status of the interlinear intermediate, however, continued to be a source of uncertainty and unease, a fact reflected in the rich flora of metaphors applied to this indirect practice in translational discourse over the period. Such translating is compared to a variety of activities implying frustration, such as "casting bullets from clay", "using a plough instead of a tractor", "turning a butterfly into a caterpillar and then trying to turn it into a butterfly again" and "resolving an equation with all unknowns" (see Witt 2013a, 164, 173). The practice was also compared to alchemy and sorcery, and even to taking a death mask from a corpse (the interlinear being a corpse).

The frustration experienced by Russian translators who depended on interlinears reached a peak following the Soviet annexation of the Baltic states in 1940. This geopolitical expansion implied an inclusion of new source literatures into the Soviet canon and created a demand for translations from Estonian, Latvian and Lithuanian. While the culture of these countries was well known and familiar to most Russians, their languages were as unintelligible and alien to them as any of the Turkic nationalities' languages, which prompted a new need for interlinear translations to be used as intermediates. As evidenced in the archival documentation from the Nationalities Commission of the Union of Soviet Writers in 1943, this situation exposed problems inherent in the practice which had not previously been perceived as such. As argued by one Lithuanian author, exiled to Moscow after the German invasion of 1941, the method had proven unsuitable in relation to Lithuanian poetry which traditionally built not on spectacular metaphors and similes but was instead distinguished by a subtle folkish language: "what sometimes may be glimpsed between the lines, what is written in the simplest words of the people, become banalities in the interlinear and such interlinears do not inspire translators; these poems get lost".[17] The epistemological dead end confronting the final translator was compared by a Russian member of the Baltic Commission to "playing a blind man's buff". Working in the field himself, he complained, referring to Nikolai Gogol's famous short story "The Nose": "It is difficult to translate from a bad interlinear. You take the interlinear and there everything comes out in a flat [trivial] way, like major Kovalev touching his nose and finding a completely flat spot."[18] As stated by Petr Skosyrev, secretary of the Board of the Nationalities Commission, in the case of "Oriental" translation (that is, from the languages of Central Asia and the Caucasus) the "unusual images and metaphors" provided sufficient material for the poet-translators, while in the case of the Baltic languages ("Western languages with foreign roots"), which lacked such conspicuous features, indirect translation was no longer acceptable.[19]

The official requirements articulated in 1943 to the effect that Russian translators orienting themselves toward the Baltic literatures were to have at least "an average command of the language"[20] seem to have had limited impact, as interlinear intermediates continued to play a significant role in this context as well. When, in 1965, there was a competition for the best translation of a poem by Lithuanian poet Salomea Neris, the source text presented to the 75 participants was not the original, but a Russian *podstrochnik* (Gasparov 2001).

Agency and regulation

The issue of translational agency – "the capacity to carry out actions" or "the willingness and ability to act" (see discussion of the term in Pym 2011) – becomes significantly more complicated in cases such as the ones described above than in cases of direct translation, for obvious reasons. As agents multiply, so do the various kinds of agency made possible at the different stages of the translation process. The Soviet archival material gives ample evidence both of initiatives taken by various agents (including authors) and of the administrative steps taken by the literary apparatus to manage the results of such activities and regulate the space open for agency. It also shows that institutional aspects of the apparatus itself could prompt certain types of initiatives.

One such aspect was the system of renumeration. The producer of the interlinear intermediate was paid only one-tenth to one-sixth of the (final) translator's fee, which, in turn, was about the same as the original author's. Thus there were strong incentives to increase the number of lines, which was the basis for calculation. As noticed by one Russian translator, such additive translation on part of the *podstrochnikist* led to a "loss of the literary style of the work"[21] and subsequently constituted another source of epistemological uncertainty inherent in the practice. The same economic interest could, of course, affect the work of the final (intralingual) translator as well. The cited translator, for example, was himself accused of having added an extra 900 lines to a Kazakh folk epic, an operation which would have generated a significant sum (Witt 2013a, 166). Such actions were made possible by another factor adding to the accumulated uncertainty of the method, namely the lack of corresponding linguistic competence on part of the editors. Work at this stage of the publishing process was almost exclusively monolingual, as a translator of Georgian origin (an example of a bilingual in this context) complained: "We don't have editors who know nationalities languages. The function of the editor is reduced to smoothing out the translation, Russifying it, thinking that he is a master who knows what the Russian should be like."[22] The idea of introducing the function of a "controller" (*svershchik*) responsible for comparing the translations with the original texts either before or after editing was endorsed by many translators, but its implementation has not been possible to assess in the material.

Economic incentives prompted the emergence of intermediate texts with quite varied status. Original authors writing in nationalities languages were strongly motivated to have their works translated into Russian, as they would then enter Soviet literature at the all-union level, with corresponding print runs (the first print often amounting to at least 10,000 copies, to be followed by possible reprints). The initiative was often taken by authors themselves by approaching individual translators or representatives of the literary apparatus in order to promote the translation of their own work into Russian, a practice which generated extensive review on the part of the Writers' Union with regard to the expertise of its nationalities cadres. Indicative of such initiatives – as well as of the procedures generally involved in the production of the bard literature – is a review produced by the Kazakh writer and literary official Abil'da Tazhibaev, dated 25 July 1940:

> At your request I have read some poems by the Kazakh bard [*akyn*] Dzhangabylev and the Dagestani bard [*ashug*] Murta-Zaliev. Dzhangabylev's poems written about Lenin, Stalin, the Kazakh folk hero Amangeldy and other poems on defense topics are not significant in any way. It is clear that the *akyn* did not work independently but under the influence of another person, who roughly told him – in a newspaper jargon – about the international situation and about the achievements of our country. Otherwise the *akyn* would not have been able to produce such a thing, as his typical traits are his imagery and the expressiveness of poetical language. In a bleak and tedious way every poem tells the "history" of Soviet

power, victories on all fronts and ends with the cliché, "We are heading towards communism." From the same "success" suffers the Dagestani *ashug* Murta-Zaliev, who has written a poem on the Red Army and Comr. Voroshilov.[23]

Agency in cases like these could perhaps be best described as fluid, involving more than one agent (cf. the constellational production referred to above). At times authors would offer *their own* interlinear intermediates in Russian without presenting the originals. Traces of such activities are, for instance, numerous archival units containing only intermediate interlinears and "literary translations" of particular works. In such cases the intermediate could technically be an original in the sense of an ultimate source text. This may be the case in the following account, given by the head of the Kazakh Commission:

> This summer [1938], I was approached by a man who said that he had a stock of Kazakh fairytales and that he could give me interlinear translations of them. I asked him to give me the originals, but he couldn't find them. I didn't accept his proposal and I was probably right in doing so, because in such cases you can always get into trouble.[24]

Massive evidence of the problems caused by the lack of originals is found in the documentation from the Nationalities Commission of the Writers' Union pertaining to the years 1939–40 (for a detailed account, see Witt 2013a). At this time the problem of originals was actualized, in particular, by the need for authoritative source-language editions of the output of the bards which had previously appeared almost exclusively in translation and mainly in newspapers. The death of Stal'skii (whose 70th anniversary in 1939 was a main reason for publication) and the advanced age of Dzhambul (born in 1846) contributed to a sense of urgency in this task, and field expeditions had been sent out to Dagestan and Kazakhstan to clarify the state of their literary legacy. In both cases alarming textological situations were reported. In Dagestan, "at the Writers' Union were discovered large amounts of absolutely illiterate *podstrochniki*, cohering neither with the original nor with common sense".[25] Over 30 works by Stal'skii published in Russian translation were found to lack any originals whatsoever, a fact presenting significant obstacles to the production of a planned volume in the original Lezgian langugage. As evidenced by the reporter, some poems could be included in this book only in the form of *back translations* from Russian. As the Russian source texts themselves had a complex genealogy, sometimes involving an Azerbaijani intermediate (Witt 2013a, 170), the ontological status of the new Lezgian – in fact, secondary – originals was utterly unclear. In the absence of ultimate source texts – which, in the case of these bards, would be transcriptions of oral performances – intermediate interlinears acquired documentary value and their treatment became a central issue in the attempts on the part of the literary apparatus to regulate the practice.[26]

Against the background of the chaotic situation which had thus been revealed, and following intense discussions at the Nationalities Commission, a resolution was passed in January 1940 which was entitled "On the Regulation of Literary Translations from the Langues of the Peoples of the USSR".[27] Here it was declared that "since the fundamental task of any translation is the re-creation, by the means of one language, of a work written in another language, it is necessary for the translator to know the language of the work he is translating", and that all organizations conducting "educational and cultural work" with writers were obliged to assist them in learning the languages of the "brotherly republics" (56). However, as such a task was time-consuming, and the "needs of the Soviet reader for literary translations from the nationalities languages have to be satisfied immediately", it was stated that "the practice of literary translation by way of organizing a preliminary interlinear translation of the original" could be allowed for as a temporary solution (57).

It was pointed out that the translator, in familiarizing himself with this interlinear, was "sort of" (*kak by*) familiarizing himself with the original. Recognizing the high demands thereby put on the intermediate, the resolution presented a list of requirements obviously designed to enhance the value of the *podstrochnik* as an epistemological tool.

First, it had to

> transfer absolutely exactly the general content of the work as well as its whole system of images, and the characteristic traits of its lexicon, while at the same time preserving the syntactical and intonational structures of the poetic language of the original author. (57)

In view of the significant differences which existed between the individual languages of the USSR, and the corresponding difficulties in translating "certain words, images and entire syntactical groups of the original", it was declared compulsory to provide the interlinear in *two* versions: one version (a word-for-word one) was to give a translation of each word in the original, retaining the word order characteristic of the original; the other (an "intelligible one") had to "open up for the translator the meaning of each phrase of the original, revealing (deciphering) each verbal complex and image which is not always clear from a literal translation" (58). In addition, the interlinear should be complemented by "a description (a scheme) of the rhythmical structure of the original with an obligatory description of the stanzaic structure, the order of caesuras, the alternation of rhymes and their characterization" (58). Furthermore, with the interlinear "the original work in Russian transcription" or a transcription into the translating language (if other than Russian) should be enclosed. It was emphasized that "without such an original the *podstrochnik* could not be accepted as the basis for a literary [*khudozhestvennyi*] translation" (58). Also to be attached was a commentary, including some "information on the author of the original work as well as on the work itself (the affiliation of the author to a literary school, the dates of composition of the works, etc.)" (58). In addition, the *podstrochnik* was to be richly commented upon from the point of view of "images, phrases and individual words which risked being misinterpreted or not understood" (58). Reaching back to Toury's distinction we may say that these requirements were oriented towards enhancing the possibilities for "translation of literary texts", as opposed to "literary translation" (1995, 168).

A further point in the resolution addressed a problem that had been widely discussed within the organization in terms of the "responsibility" of the translator. It was stated that the interlinear "could not and should not be anonymous": "The existence of the signature of the author (or the authors) of the interlinear translation is a condition without which this interlinear translation could not be used for work" (58–59). The make-up of this specific group of agents was declared an issue of particular importance, subject to administrative efforts on the part of the apparatus:

> Since the making of intermediate interlinears is serious and responsible work, requiring from the author good knowledge of languages as well as literary taste and a considerable amount of culture, the Board of every writers' organization in the republics and regions is obliged to carry out registration of these cadres and draw them into the daily creative work of the writers' collective. It is inadmissible to entrust the making of intermediate interlinears to random people who are not able to bear responsibility for the work they have been assigned. (59)

Bearing in mind the enormous quantities of text that had to be processed according to the rules proposed in the resolution, it is possible to perceive the truly utopian dimension of this document, which was in a sense typical of Soviet projects in general. A point in the practical part of the resolution contributed significantly to its utopian character, suggesting that the Gorky Institute of World Literature in Moscow (an institution within the structure of the Soviet Academy of Sciences) set up an "all-Union scholarly archive" comprising "all materials relating to the literary translation from the languages of the peoples of the USSR" (60). The archive was to receive "copies of all intermediate interlinears produced locally as well as in Moscow". In this way, it was declared, the new archive would constitute "not only the main depository for all material concerning translations but also a kind of central control instance for issues relating to translation from the literatures of the peoples of the USSR" (60–61). Although the impact of the resolution is difficult to assess (no traces of such an archive have been localized at the institution mentioned here), the utopian ambition continued to be reflected in the documentation of the Nationalities Commission. For example, a working plan for the year 1944 included the following far-reaching item, indicating the importance of intermediates in the administration of Soviet literature as a multinational product: "Reprinting (in collotype press) of intermediate interlinears of all famous literary works of the peoples of the USSR for distribution to all national republics of the USSR."[28]

A specific function accorded the intermediate interlinears had a bearing on issues of censorship. While translation itself on a general level could be viewed as a complex set of censorial practices – from the choice of works to be translated to the methods applied (cf. Sherry 2015) – prose interlinears played a specific role in the editorial processing of the enormous amounts of text involved. Apart from giving a hint about the quality of a particular work, they offered the editor an opportunity to reject politically unacceptable texts at an early stage, before wasting money on the final translation. As one editor commented:

> From the *podstrochnik* I can see if it is necessary to translate a piece or not. There was an incident with Comr. Minikh. He brought a poem from the Tatar republic. It was a good lyrical poem, but it had a flaw: the author juxtaposed the individual and the societal. If I had had a *podstrochnik* I could have said immediately that it was not to be translated. His hero finds himself in the army and writes a letter to his girl … . Further on he makes a political mistake. He writes to her that he is at the front, very far away, and that letters do not reach them there. That is slander. When the events at the lake Khazan happened the commanders and the commissars wrote to the families of the soldiers and told them of their heroic deeds. That's how you should work with *podstrochniki*.[29]

Despite the theoretical and organizational efforts thus put into the Soviet system of indirect translation, it seems largely to have resisted improvements.[30] Contrary to all declarations of its temporary character, it continued to prosper. In his seminal work *Foundations for a General Theory of Translation*, Andrei Fedorov comments on the practice as "an essential defect" which had been affecting nationalities translation and which "had not yet been overcome":

> The podstrochnik is an eccentric, often monstrous phenomenon, in which it is necessary to combine both a striving toward literalism (since the translating person has to know all the elements of the text) and toward meaning; oftentimes this is not achieved, because the one excludes the other. (1968, 125)

In 1972, a reviewer of a new edition of a Kazakh poet made from intermediate interlinears criticized a range of shortcomings, including the anonymity of the compilers. He concluded: "The *Selected Works* of Sultanmakhmut Toraigyrov is a most vivid example of HOW NOT to issue the poems by a canonical writer who is the pride of his national culture" (Zhovtis 1972, 118). As for the means of regulation, it was not until 1987 that a rule was imposed that prohibited the publication of translations of work which had not been published in their original langugage (Goble 1990, 138), presumably putting an end to the problem of the *podstrochnik* as an "original genre", lacking an identifiable source text.

Conclusion

The overview of issues relating to Soviet practices of indirect translation provided in this article gives strong support to the claim that "[t]he study of a translation without information about the ways in which it has come into being – directly or with the help of an intermediate interlinear – is either impossible or idle" (Vanechkova 1978, 12). It is clear that research on translation in the USSR has to confront a complex reality which is seldom reflected in reference works or bibliographies. This is a fact that complicates large-scale projects aiming to study, for example, translation flows within the Union and centre–periphery relations.

The final outcome of the massive use of intermediate texts for translation in Soviet culture was multifaceted and paradoxical. It installed a specific epistemological uncertainty into large parts of the literary system, while simultaneously calling attention to the mediated nature of all text production in Soviet culture, involving editors, correctors, censors, etc. It relativized the very concept of translation, and, perhaps even more importantly, of the translator, continuously informing discourses of professionalization and status. It produced new types of translational agency and new types of texts with varying ontological status.

The persistence of the practice, despite educational efforts on the part of all the agents of translation – authors, *podstrochnikisty*, final translators and editors – suggests that it was in fact a vital constituent of the mode of functioning of the multinational but Russocentric Soviet literature. The Soviet efforts to perfect the method of *podstrochnik* translation, preferring it to relay translation, at least in theory, may recall the utopianist mode of Walter Benjamin's rejection of "translations made from translations" in favour of "the interlinear version of the Scriptures" as "the prototype or ideal of all translation" (Benjamin 2004, 83).

Notes

1. Russian State Archive for Literature and Art [RGALI], f. 631, op. 6, ed. khr. 294, l. 13. All translations in this article are mine (S.W.) if not otherwise indicated.
2. The extent to which intermediate interlinears were used in translation of non-literary texts still remains to be explored; such translation is, as a rule, not reflected in the archival documentation pertaining to the Soviet Writers' Union.
3. The Nationalities Commission was a body assigned the task of "mutual and broad familiarization with the literatures of the brotherly republics", at the heart of which was translation. (RGALI, f. 631, op. 6, ed. khr. 295, l. 1). In particular, its work was to further the publication

of nationalities literature in Russian, thereby giving it access to the "arena of world literature" (RGALI, f. 631, op. 6, ed. khr. 295, l. 2). Within its structure were subdivisions such as the Kazakh Commission, the Dagestani Commission, etc.

4. The boom was of course also a result of state and party initiatives, such as the 1935 "Resolution of the Presidium of the Nationalities Council of the Central Executive Committee of the USSR on the Development of Artistic Creation on Part of the Peoples of the USSR" (RGALI, f. 613, op. 1, ed. khr. 4719).

5. RGALI, f. 631, op. 6, ed. khr. 425. A certain fatigue among the officials may be glimpsed through the archival material: "The procession of jubilees which has been set in motion all over the Soviet land is an indicator of the genuine growth of the cultures of the Soviet people. … However, if people try to invent causes for a jubilee in an artificial way, this is already a dangerous thing" (Skosyrev, RGALI, f. 631, op. 6, ed. khr. 295, l. 30).

6. Pseudotranslation as defined by Toury himself is "texts which have been presented as translations with no corresponding source texts in other languages ever having existed – hence no factual 'transfer operations' and translation relationships" (1995, 40).

7. RGALI, f. 631, op. 6, ed. khr. 230.

8. Although a possible case, the *podstrochnik* was very seldom "a textually-dominated translation", yielding "products which are well-formed in terms of general conventions of text formation pertinent to the target culture, even if they do not conform to any recognized literary model within it" (Toury 1995, 171). In many cases, the qualifier "well-formed" did not apply even at the linguistic level.

9. RGALI, f. 631, op. 21, ed. khr. 1, l. 24. Detailing the existing professional qualifications among Soviet translators in the early 1930s, the report provides a virtual snapshot of the whole situation in the field of literary translation at the time.

10. RGALI, f. 631, op. 21, ed. khr. 1, ll. 11–12.

11. The career of Ezra Levontin (1891–1968) is quite representative of the category of poet-translator (*poet-perevodchik*) in the Soviet literary system: having authored several collections of original poetry (far from a proletarian kind) prior to 1928, he could publish mainly as a translator from nationalities langugages (Kazakh, Chechen and Mari, a Finno-Ugric language spoken in parts of Eastern Russia); occasionally he published translations of Western authors such as Guy de Maupassant (see e.g. http://www.vekperevoda.com/1887/levont. htm) and some translation criticism.

12. RGALI, f. 631, op. 21, ed. khr. 7, l. 4; here, the applicant is called a "translator" in quotation marks.

13. RGALI, f. 631, op. 21, ed. khr. 22, l. 8.

14. Initiatives taken by the Translators' Section to further direct translation include the following activities reported in 1936: "The Section has organized two-year seminars at the Literary University [at the Writers' Union] in the art of translation from English, German and French. They are now running successfully in their second year. Currently they are being complemented by seminars on translation from Ukrainian, Georgian, and Turkic langugages, which occupies a prominent place within the literature of the peoples of the USSR while at the same time experiencing a lack of translators (into Russian) (RGALI, f. 631, op. 21, ed. khr. 12, l. 26).

15. RGALI, f. 631, op. 21, ed. khr. 5, l. 21 (Rozaliia Shor).

16. RGALI, f. 631, op. 21, ed. khr. 5, l. 76. The case of Osip Kolychev (1904–73) differs from that of Levontin: translation was not a substitute but a complement to his career as an original, well-published Stalinist poet. Examples of this category were quite numerous as well.

17. RGALI, f. 631, op. 6, ed. khr. 657, l. 69 (Kostas Korsakas; see Witt 2013a for the context of this discussion).

18. RGALI, f. 631, op. 6, ed. khr. 659, l. 32 (Mikhail Zenkevich).

19. RGALI, f. 631, op. 6, ed. khr. 657, l. 86.

20. RGALI, f. 631, op. 6, ed. khr. 657, l. 86.

21. RGALI, f. 631, op. 21, ed. khr. 1, l. 33 (Lev Pen'kovskii, 1934).

22. RGALI, f. 631, op. 21, ed. khr. 23, l. 21 (Elena Gogoberidze, 1938).

23. RGALI, f. 631, op. 6, ed. khr. 512, l. 14. It is a fact that many of the works of "nationalities authors" that were actually published could be described in a similar way. Tazhibaev was himself one of the poets engaged in the project of transcribing the oral works of Dzhambul and providing intermediate interlinears, as described above.

24. RGALI, f. 631, op. 6, ed. khr. 295, l. 6 (Leonid Sobolev, 1939).

25. RGALI, f. 631, op. 6, ed. khr. 294, l. 2 (Evgenii Korabel'nikov, 1939).

26. The problem had been officially recognized already at the First All-Union Conference of Translators in 1936, the resolution of which stated, with reference to the intermediate interlinears, "[n]oting the extremely low quality of *podstrochniki* and the howling examples of distortions and ad-libbing [*otsebiatina*] in translation from the nationalities languages into Russian, it should be suggested to publishing houses that they raise their demands in terms of the quality of their *podstrochniki* and, with the aim of attracting highly qualified cadres, at the same time increase the payment offered to *podstrochniki* as much as possible" (RGALI, f. 631, op. 21, ed. khr. 9, ll. 1–2; see also Witt 2013b). The impact of this suggestion had apparently been insignificant.

27. RGALI, f. 631, op. 6, ed. khr. 475, ll. 56–61 (original text published in Witt 2013a). In the following, in-text references will be given to sheets (*listy*) in this document.

28. RGALI, f. 631, op. 6, ed. khr. 696, l. 2. The points of the 1940 resolution were elaborated further in the article "Literary Translation and Its Portfolio", written at the request of the Nationalities Commission by the poet-translator Mark Tarlovskii (1940) and published in the periodical anthology *Druzhba narodov* (Peoples' friendship), which had been founded in 1939 with a view to providing an "organizational basis for finally settling the problem of translations" (RGALI, f. 631, op. 6, ed. khr. 308, l. 7). For more on Tarlovskii's article, see Witt 2011, 161–162.

29. RGALI, f. 631, op. 6, ed. khr. 308, l. 33 (Deev 1939).

30. It should be pointed out, however, that the quality of the intermediate texts could differ significantly: "There are *podstrochniki* from which the [final] translator picks not only images and individual words but which often provide entire groups of words or even lines. And then there are such *podstrochniki* with which the [final] translator has to struggle, seeking out other expressions than the ones used in them" (Khachatriants 1939, 4). For a case of *podstrochnik* translation involving both an original text, an annotated interlinear and some contextual information, recalling the requirements as described above, see Witt 2015.

Disclosure statement

No potential conflict of interest was reported by the author.

Funding

This work was supported by Vetenskapsrådet: [Grant Number 2014-1187].

References

Antokol'skii, Pavel, Mukhtar Auezov, and Maksim Ryl'skii. 1955. "Khudozhe stvennye perevody literatur narodov SSSR [Translations from the literatures of the peoples of USSR]." In *Voprosy khudozhestvennogo perevoda* [Problems of literary translation], edited by Vladimir Rossel's, 5–44. Moscow: Sovetskii pisatel'.

Bagno, Vsevolod, and Nikolai Kazanskii. 2011. "Die zeitgenössische russische Übersetzung, ihre Rolle in Russlands internationaler Verortung und bei der russischen Aneignung der Weltkultur [Contemporary Russian translation, its role in Russia's international position and in Russian appropriation of world culture]." In *Übersetzung: ein internationales Handbuch zur Übersetzungsforschung* [Translation: an international encyclopedia of translation studies], edited by Harald Kittel et al., vol. 3, 2082–2090. Berlin: de Gruyter.

Benjamin, Walter. 2004 [1923]. "The Task of the Translator. An Introduction to the Translation of Baudelaire's Tableaux Parisiens." In *The Translation Studies Reader*, Translated by Harry Zohn. edited by Lawrence Venuti, 2nd ed., 75–83. New York and London: Routledge.

Dollerup, Cay. 2000. "Relay and Support Translations." In *Translation in Context*, edited by Andrew Chesterman, Natividad Gallardo San Salvador, and Yves Gambier, 17–26. Amsterdam: John Benjamins.

Even Zohar, Itamar. 2008. "Culture Planning, Cohesion, and the Making and Maintenance of Entities." In *Beyond Descriptive Translation Studies: Investigations in Homage to Gideon Toury*, edited by Anthony Pym, Miriam Shlesinger, and Daniel Simeoni, 277–292. Amsterdam: John Benjamins.

Gasparov, Mikhail. 2001. "Podstrochnik i mera tochnosti [The interlinear and the measure of accuracy]." In *O russkoi poezii. Analizy. Interpretatsii. Kharakteristiki* [On Russian poetry. Analyses. Interpretations. Characteristics], 363–372. Moscow: Azbuka.

Goble, Paul A. 1990. "Readers, Writers and Republics: The Structural Basis of Non-Russian Literary Politics." In *The Nationalitites Factor in Soviet Politics and Society*, edited by Lubomyr Hajda and Mark Beissinger, 131–147. Oxford: Westview.

Grenoble, Lenore. 2003. *Language Policy in the Soviet Union*. Dordrecht: Kluwer Academic.

Jakobson, Roman. 1959. "On Linguistic Aspects of Translation." In *On Translation*, edited by Reuben Brower, 232–239. Cambridge, MA: Harvard University.

Khachatriants, Iakov. 1939. "O podstrochnikakh [On interlinears]." *Literaturnaia gazeta* 54, September 30: 4.

Kittel, Harald, and Armin Paul Frank, eds. 1991. *Interculturality and the Historical Study of Literary Translations*. Berlin: Erich Schmidt Verlag.

Milton, John, and Paul F. Bandia. 2009. "Introduction: Agents of Translation and Translation Studies." In *Agents of Translation*, edited by John Milton and Paul F. Bandia, 1–17. Amsterdam: Benjamins.

Pechat' SSSR=Pechat' SSSR za sorok let 1917–1957. Statisticheskie materialy [Publishing in the USSR during 40 years 1917–1957]. Moscow: 1957.

Pervyi s"ezd [First congress]=Luppol, L.K, M. M. Rozental' and S. M. Tretiakov (eds.). 1990. *Pervyi vsesoiuznyi s"ezd sovetskikh pisatelei 1934, stenograficheskii otchet* [First all-Union congress of Soviet writers 1934, stenographic report]. Moscow: Sovetskii pisatel'.

Ringmar, Martin. 2007. "'Roundabout Routes': Some Remarks on Indirect Translations." In *Selected Papers of the CETRA Research Seminar in Traslation Studies* 2006, edited by Francis Mus. Accessed January 14, 2016. http://www2.arts.kuleuven.be/cetra/papers/Papers2006/RINGMAR.pdf.

Russian State Archive for Literature and Art (RGALI), fond 631 (Union of Soviet Writers), opis' 6 (Nationalities Commission); opis' 21 (Translators' Section).

Schultze, Brigitte. 2014. "Historical and systematical aspects of indirect translation in the de Gruyter Handbuch Übersetzung —HSK. 26.1–3: insight and impulse to further research." *Zeitschrift für Slawistik* 59 (4): 507–528.

Sherry, Samantha. 2015. *Discourses of Regulation and Resistance: Censoring Translation in the Stalin and Khrushchev Era Soviet Union*. Edinburgh: Edinburgh University.

Tarlovskii, Mark. 1940. "Khudozhestvennyi perevod i ego portfel'[Literary translation and its portfolio]." *Druzhba narodov* 4: 263–284.

Toury, Gideon. 1995. *Descriptive Translation Studies and Beyond*. Amsterdam: Benjamins.

Toury, Gideon. 2005. "Enhancing cultural changes by means of fictitious translation." In *Translation and Cultural Change: Studies in history, norms and image-projection*, edited by Eva Hung, 3–17. Amsterdam: Benjamins.

Vanechkova, Galina. 1978. "Podstrochnik — posrednik mezhdu avtorom i perevodchikom [The interlinear — an intermediate between author and translator]." *Československá rusistika* XXIII (1): 10–14.

Witt, Susanna. 2011. "Between the Lines: Totalitarianism and Translation in the USSR." In *Contexts, Subtexts and Pretexts: Literary Translation in Eastern Europe and Russia*, edited by Brian James Baer, 149–170. Amsterdam: John Benjamins.

Witt, Susanna. 2013a. "The Shorthand of Empire: Podstrochnik Practices and the Making of Soviet Literature." *Ab Imperio: Studies of New Imperial History and Nationalism in the post-Soviet Space* 14 (3): 155–190.

Witt, Susanna. 2013b. "Arts of Accommodation: The First All-Union Conference of Translators, Moscow, 1936, and the Ideologization of Norms." In *The Art of Accommodation: Literary Translation in Russia*, edited by Leon Burnett and Emily Lygo, 141–184. Oxford: Peter Lang.

Witt, Susanna. 2015. "Pasternak, Łysohorsky and the Significance of "Unheroic" Translation." *Russian Literature* 78 (3–4): 755–773.

Zaborov, Petr. 1963. "'literatura-posrednik' v istorii russko-zapadnykh literaturnykh sviazei XVII–XIX vv. ['The mediating literature' in the history of Russian-Western literary relations]" In *Mezhdunarodnye sviazi russkoi literatury* [International relations of Russian literature], edited by Mikhail P. Alekseev, 64–85. Moscow–Leningrad: Izdatel'stvo Akademii Nauk.

Zaborov, Petr. 2011. "Die Zwischenübersetzung in der Geschichte der russischen Literatur [The intermediate translation in the history of Russian literature]." In *Übersetzung. Translation. Traduction*, edited by Harald Kittel, vol. 3, 2066–2073. Berlin: Walter de Gruyter.

Zemskova, Elena. 2013. "Translators in the Soviet Writers' Union: Pasternak's Translations from Georgian Poets and the Literary Process of the Mid-1930s." In *The Art of Accommodation: Literary Translation in Russia*, edited by Leon Burnett and Emily Lygo, 185–212. Oxford: Peter Lang.

Zhovtis, Aleksandr. 1972. "Poeziia, podstrochnik, perevod: lirika Toraigyrova v novom russkom izdanii [Poetry, interlinear, translation: the lyric poetry of Toraigyrov in a new Russian edition]." *Prostor* 4: 114–118.

Indirect translation and discursive identity: Proposing the concatenation effect hypothesis

James Hadley ●

ABSTRACT
This article posits the hypothesis that indirect translations are predisposed to limit both their acknowledgement of their cultural alterity, and the inclusion of elements particular to the source culture. Basing its argument on the discursive identity spectrum proposed by Clem Robyns, this article argues that the likelihood of such cultural specificities being omitted or replaced is extremely high in indirect translations, as a result of a phenomenon termed the "concatenation effect". The article synthesizes the discursive identity spectrum with a meta-analysis approach, focusing on literary examples taken from a variety of cultural contexts, in order to illustrate the generalized nature of its hypothesis. This hypothesis offers a new framework for the analysis of indirect translations, nuanced beyond traditional dualities, and observable among multiple translating cultures.

The aim of this article is to posit the hypothesis that indirect translations exhibit a proclivity towards omitting cultural elements particular to their source cultures, and also towards downplaying the foreign origins of their source texts. An indirect translation here is conceptualized as a translation that uses another translation as its source text. Important for this study is the assumption that each translation is produced on its own terms, and so the first translation is not produced in order to facilitate the production of a subsequent translation, but exists as a target text in its own right for its own target culture. The article will adopt the discursive identity spectrum, posited by Clem Robyns (1994), as its theoretical apparatus. On this spectrum, Robyns (ibid., 408–409) identifies four initial "stands" a translator or translating culture may potentially take towards its sources. Using Robyns' spectrum as a framework, this article's style will be primarily meta-analytical in the sense that it will rely on extant scholarship into each stage of the translation process, as opposed to performing textual analysis directly. This approach will allow the article to make its findings as context-neutral as possible by observing the described phenomenon in a variety of linguistic, cultural and historical contexts. The aim of this context-neutrality is to reduce the likelihood that the posited hypothesis is heavily language- or culture-specific.

Through this analysis, the aim will be to illustrate the hypothesis that largely irrespective of the individual translators' stands or translation strategies, acts of indirect translation are highly prone to tend towards what Robyns' (ibid., 408) terminology describes as an *imperialist stand*. This tendency toward the omission of the cultural other and the disregarding of this other is termed here "the concatenation effect", which describes translators' stands influencing one another directly, such that translated texts come to resemble those produced in stands not ascribed to by any of the translators.

The discursive identity spectrum

Robyns conceptualizes discursive identity as it relates to translation in terms of a spectrum of attitudes or "stands" that a translator or translating culture may take towards a source or source culture. His paradigm, and the four points on the spectrum he describes, pivot on two Boolean parameters, which are whether or not the alterity of a source text or the culture it represents is acknowledged by a translator or translating culture, and whether or not cultural particularities of the source text or source culture are permitted to permeate the translation. Based on the binary nature of these two parameters, Robyns identifies four possible points on the spectrum, termed the *defective stand*, the *trans-discursive stand*, the *defensive stand* and the *imperialistic stand*.

The *defective stand* describes translations which actively acknowledge the foreign origins of source texts and also retain foreign elements within them (ibid., 409). Robyns (420–421) draws on post-war period France, when the detective novel genre, which had previously developed a notable discrepancy between the French literary system and its British and American counterparts, began importing the genre in its anglophone guise. Robyns (423) notes that translations went on to dominate the genre in France until the late 1960s, with 75% of the texts having been translated from English. Robyns (423) generalizes that, in a *defective stand*, a system will tend to perceive translations in enriching terms, and therefore not as intrinsically incompatible with native discourse. Thus, overtly foreign features or characteristics of texts can be accepted as such by the target culture, because it acknowledges the texts themselves as overtly foreign.

The *trans-discursive stand*, on the other hand, describes translation activities which retain foreign elements without emphasizing them, or the texts themselves, as intrinsically foreign (ibid., 418). Robyns draws on contemporary Dutch contexts to illustrate this stand. He describes the detached, pragmatic attitude with which the status of the Dutch language has been approached in many cases in recent history, drawing on the example of the Dutch education minister's suggestion that English be made the primary language of instruction in Dutch universities (417–419). Robyns asserts that counter-arguments were not chiefly centred on any presumed primacy of the Dutch language or appeals to sentiments regarding what could be seen as the demotion of the national language, because the English language in this case was not perceived as representing the alien (418).

The *defensive stand* is the inverse of the *trans-discursive stand*. It describes translations which acknowledge texts' foreign origins but do not retain any foreign elements (ibid., 415, 417). Robyns (414–417) illustrates this stand through the example of the Québecois attitude towards the English language, which is frequently framed in threatening terms.

He compares this threatening presence with the status of French-language materials from other francophone contexts, which are perceived as threatening only in their spoken forms (415). Robyns (415) demonstrates that a *defensive stand* implies an acknowledgement and even an emphasis of the foreign origins of a discourse, in order to bring its contrast with the domestic discourse into sharper relief. However, in the process of translating, such a stand will also routinely remove any elements that do not correspond closely with this native discourse, eliminating the essentially foreign nature of the text (417).

The *imperialist stand* is the last point in Robyns' description of the discursive identity spectrum (ibid., 409). It is the opposite of the *defective stand* in that it describes translations that neither acknowledge the foreign origins of their source texts nor retain foreign elements from them. Here, Robyns (410–413) draws on the example of the traditional, and institutionalized, though paradoxical French position that the francophone system is universal, and simultaneously superior to all rivals. He shows that, in *imperialist* systems, the supposed universality of the domestic discourse leads translations to be viewed as transparent proxies for their source texts, although, in real terms, translations often acquire heavily transformative functions, with foreign features being adapted or omitted (413). Thus, within an *imperialist stand*, translations exhibit both a lack of acknowledgement of the other and a rejection of features that might be equated with alterity.

Robyns does not conceptualize these four stands as mutually exclusive, or as a complete taxonomy. Rather, he acknowledges that "no discourse will ever correspond exactly to a single type", and likewise that no "discourse [will] ever reflect only one attitude" (ibid., 409). This article and its hypothesis, which employs the stands Robyns describes in the same proximate manner, embrace his acknowledgement of a lack of absolutes. However, where Robyns' focus is on the description of whole contexts, or literary systems as they relate to others, the focus of this article falls on individual texts. Hence, Robyns' stands will not be interpreted here as indicative or representative of anything beyond the relationship individual translators and their translations exhibit towards their source texts and source cultures.

The article's intention is not to argue that all indirect translations are maximally, uniformly or even equally *imperialist*. Rather, it posits the hypothesis that indirect translations are likely to be more closely comparable with an *imperialist stand* than any of the other four stands described above. This hypothesis is based on the reasoning that translations produced from texts that are also translations, and with no direct reference to those translations' sources, are inherently constrained by the stands and strategies taken by the first translations. Since it acts as a source to the second translation, the stand towards the source text or its culture taken by a first translation will inevitably have a repercussive effect on any translation subsequently based on it. If the first translation fails to acknowledge the foreign origins of the source text, subsequent translations' abilities to do so will be reduced. Similarly, if the first translation fails to retain any features that are culturally specific to the source text, subsequent translations' abilities to do so will be reduced. Hence, it can be predicted that only in the case of both translators taking a *defective stand* is the final translation likely both to acknowledge the foreign nature of the source text and to retain cultural particularities of it.

It should be acknowledged that it is overly simplistic to imagine all translators working from sources that are also translations having no access to alternative sources of information on textual and cultural particularities relevant to the text in question. It is possible that translators who are aware of the ultimate source from which a text is derived may encounter alternative translations, or read translations of similar texts, and subsequently may choose to introduce culturally specific features indicative of this source setting, as part of their own translation strategies. Doing so would tend to reduce such a text's overall proximity on the discursive identity spectrum to the *imperialist stand*. However, it remains to be seen whether such indirectly added features can reliably be aligned with the features found within the ultimate source text and, hence, whether they truly constitute elements of the source text, or are merely target-culture-imposed interpretations of the source culture, and therefore remain intrinsically *imperialist*.

Case 1: Classical Chinese-French-Portuguese

An example of an indirect translation taking on an *imperialist stand*, as a result of the concatenating effect of the two translators involved, can be found in Antônio Feijó's *Cancioneiro Chinez* (1890), a Portuguese translation of Judith Gautier's *Livre de Jade* (1869), which is one of the earliest anthologies of Classical Chinese poetry in French translation (Yu 2007a, 220).

Le Livre de Jade appeared at a time when the view of Abel Rémusat, one of Europe's leading Sinologists, was that Classical Chinese poetry was at best untranslatable and at worst incomprehensible (Yu 2007b, 467). Gautier, the daughter of novelist and literary critic Théophile Gautier, undertook the translation of a large corpus of this work at the age of 24, after four years of study under Ding Dunling [丁敦齡] (Yu 2007a, 219). Gautier and Ding relied on the collection of Chinese manuscripts held by the Bibliothèque Impériale as the source for much of the anthology, though Ding is also named as the author of numerous poems in the anthology (Hamao 1995, 85; Yu 2007b, 467). For this reason, the *Livre de Jade* can be considered a collection of Classical Chinese poetry in the sense of the shared poetic idiom and style of the source texts, as opposed to a common author or period of composition.

If the sentiments of Rémusat above regarding the notional inscrutability of Classical Chinese poetry can be taken as representative of the widely held opinion of the time, it appears to foreground the *defensive stand* taken by Gautier in this translation, by framing Classical Chinese poetry as something fundamentally incompatible with both the French literary system and the French language. Indeed, Gautier's *defensive stand* and its tendency to present the translation as being intrinsically alien, with no commonalities with native genres, can be seen throughout her text. Scholars of her work have frequently noted that many of the poems in the collection cannot be aligned directly with any identifiable Classical Chinese source, and even that several of the attributions provided by Gautier are flawed (Hamao 1995, 83). For example, Yu (2007b, 468) notes that the Chinese characters used as part of the book's system of attribution are occasionally mismatched, and even that the characters of Du Fu's name [杜甫] are printed upside-down on one page. This misapplication or confusion of the respective Chinese characters demonstrates that their intended use was more decorative than informative. Judging from the early stages of Sinology in Europe at the time, it is clear that at the point when Gautier produced the translation, the number of target-language readers who would have found any meaning at all in the Chinese characters was extremely small. Hence, the inclusion of these characters, it can be assumed, occurred for reasons other than their potentially informative function for this tiny minority. Instead, the Chinese characters lent Gautier's work a sense of authority, authenticity and exoticism, explicitly emphasizing the foreign nature of the texts themselves in the minds of readers.

The fact that many of the poems in the collection have, in fact, no identifiable source in the Classical Chinese poetic canon, however, demonstrates that Gautier's main goal was to be seen to translate the work, as opposed to produce translations that were comprehensive representations of their sources. Moreover, since the source poetry had already been conceptualized as something incompatible with the French literary system, it is logical that Gautier's approach was one that foregrounded this innate foreignness, though it also resisted the importation of tangible cultural peculiarities of the source text or its literary tradition.

The 1867 edition of the book is organized into seven sections: Les Amoureux [Lovers], La Lune [The Moon], L'Automne [Autumn], Les Voyageurs [Travellers], Le Vin [Wine], La Guerre [War] and Les Poëtes [Poets] (Yoshikawa 2010, 21). By far the largest section is the first, which cannot be considered a typical theme in collections of Classical Chinese poetry (Yu 2007b, 469). Similarly, Gautier's translations of the various poems' titles almost uniformly bear no relationship to the titles of their respective source texts (Yoshikawa 2010, 20). She also routinely omits all direct references to named individuals or locations within the poems, elements that could only be perceived as exotic to the French language (Yu 2007b, 473). Moreover, Gautier's translation strategy is one that frequently translates only a part of each poem (Hamao 1995, 85; Yu 2007a, 221). Very often, her texts consist only of the first few lines of a particular poem, which frequently occur in a different order from those in her source text (Yoshikawa 2010, 22). Conjecture has historically tended to assume that these structural discrepancies occurred as a result of Gautier's incomplete grasp of the source language and its poetic idiom (Yu 2007a, 221). However, an alternative interpretation would suggest that recreating or reflecting the form or substance of the source poems was of far lower priority to Gautier than exhibiting the fact that she was translating from the Classical Chinese poetic idiom.

These manifold factors, all of which tend to omit elements alien to the French language or literary system while underscoring the source text's nature as fundamentally foreign, culminate to classify Gautier's translation stand as *defensive*. It may be that her linguistic and contextual competences with the Classical Chinese poetic idiom were factors which influenced her translations. However, such competences do not necessarily explain her omission of specifically Chinese features such as names, or the rearrangement of the poems' structures. On the other hand, if, as is suggested here, the primary goal for Gautier was to produce a translation which was seen as such, it was not necessary for her also to include encyclopaedic details, or even to translate the texts in full.

Possibly as a result of the nature of the texts themselves, or possibly because of the acclaim that Gautier garnered through translating them, *Le Livre de Jade* became extremely popular around Europe and was itself translated into a variety of other languages (Yu 2007a, 218). One such translation rendered the work into Portuguese under the title *Cancioneiro Chinez*. This translation was produced by Portuguese poet Antônio Feijó and published soon after the latter's arrival in Brazil (Martins 2011, 119).

Though this translation used Gautier's text as its source, Feijó's stand appears to be diametrically opposed to the one exhibited by Gautier, which it also inherits.

Whereas Gautier had gone to the effort of including Chinese characters in the first edition of her translation in a manner that appears to function more to remind readers of the exotic origins of the text than to serve any informative role, Feijó omits such explicit indications of the text's foreign nature, and even refrains from describing the text at any point as a translation (Pinto 2013, 64). For his part, Feijó appears to have esteemed translation as a form of cultural enrichment of the Portuguese literary system. However, such enrichment does not necessarily need to be perceived as originating outside the same literary system, and, as a result of his systematic de-emphasis of the foreign nature of the text, much of Feijó's original readership appears to have missed the implicit indications of its alterity (Pinto 2013, 64).

However, Feijó's strategy was open to including features particular to the Classical Chinese poetic idiom in a manner that is quite opposed to Gautier's. Feijó is reported to have taken some six years to produce his translation of Gautier's work, during which he read widely on the subject of Chinese literature (Pinto 2013, 71). Quite possibly as a result of this research, instead of employing Gautier's idiosyncratic organization of the various poems, discussed above, Feijó organizes them into a season-based schema of four parts that is frequently seen in the context of East Asian poetry (Pinto 2013, 67). He also does not translate all the texts contained in Gautier's collection, focusing instead predominantly on poems with identifiable sources from the Tang dynasty (Pinto 2013, 66). Hence, in restricting itself to poems first composed in medieval China, to the exclusion of the later poems that were simply written in the same style, Feijó's translation is arguably a more concentrated treatment of the same medieval Chinese tradition than Gautier's.

Conversely, whereas Gautier's translation actively distinguishes itself from the native French literary system, Feijó's translation identifies itself explicitly with the native Portuguese literary tradition from the outset. Feijó emphasizes the theme of lovers, already predominant in Gautier's translation, and translates more of the poems classified as such by Gautier than any of her other themes by a factor of at least two (Pinto 2013, 67). This focus on lovers is part of Feijó's continuous and explicit linking of his translation to the medieval Galician-Portuguese literary system (Pinto 2013, 65). By titling itself a "Cancioneiro" [songbook], Feijó's text is linked with the medieval Galician-Portuguese tradition of anthologizing poems with cognate themes. In line with this tradition, Feijó renders the prose translations Gautier had produced into regular decasyllabic quatrain, even applying a uniform a-b-a-b rhyme scheme to them (Pinto 2013, 69).

Thus, Feijó's translation inherited Gautier's *defensive stand* towards the translation of Classical Chinese poetry. While it does exhibit an interest in challenging this *defensive stand* by exploring the subject of Chinese poetry from other sources, his translation eliminates all the elements indicative of the foreign origins of the text Gautier had included. It also implicitly links the collection with a native tradition, rendering the text in accordance with historical precedent drawn from within the Portuguese literary tradition. Moreover, Feijó neglects to identify his text explicitly as a translation, and, as a result, much of his readership ultimately assumes the text to be one of Feijó's own compositions (Pinto 2013, 64).

Thus, Feijó's *trans-discursive stand* acts to downplay the sense of the text as being intrinsically foreign, though it works to retain foreign elements. However, its ability to include such elements is heavily limited by Gautier's earlier *defensive stand*. As a result, elements that can be perceived as being specific to the Chinese context, rather than the Portuguese, are minor and could easily be misidentified as authorial creativity, since their Chinese origins are not explicitly illustrated. Hence, although neither Gautier's nor Feijó's stand is *imperialist* from the outset, Feijó's translation was widely accepted as his own work and not as a translation, and he was able to include a small number of superficial elements derived tangentially from the Chinese source culture. Thus, his own *trans-discursive stand* is concatenated with Gautier's *defensive stand*, and the ultimate result is a translation that most closely compares with the *imperialist stand*.

Case 2: German-English-Japanese

This concatenating effect is by no means restricted to translations travelling from east to west. A very similar phenomenon can be observed in translations moving in the opposite direction, such as the Japanese text 西洋古事・神仙叢話 (The Ancient West: A Collection of Supernatural Stories; 1887) by Suga Ryōhō [菅了法], which is a translation from Susannah Mary Paull's *The Grimm's Fairy Tales* (1868), an English translation of Jacob and Wilhelm Grimm's *Kinder- und Hausmärchen* (1812).

Jacob and Wilhelm Grimm produced their collection of stories in line with their German Romantic nationalist ideology. They sought to collect and preserve a narrative tradition untouched by foreign influence that was representative of the German "Volksgeist" (Schacker 2003, 2). Their collection of folk tales, originally numbering 86 stories, was published as *Kinder- und Hausmärchen* in 1812, and was continuously altered and augmented over the course of the following 4 decades, with the seventh edition, published in 1857, containing some 211 tales (Morgan 2006, 1). As is well documented, the Grimms' collections, especially in their early editions, were heavily criticized for targeting juvenile readers while containing elements that were widely considered inappropriate for children (Kyritsi 2004).

Nonetheless, and in spite of the nationalistic ideology that underpinned the Grimms' story collection, their work proved extremely popular abroad, being translated widely. Translations into English ensued almost immediately after the publication of the first edition, which coincided with a dramatic upsurge in the publication of traditional tales in England (Alderson 1993, 62). The first complete translation of the tales was produced by Edgar Taylor as *German Popular Stories*, which appeared in 1826 (Alderson 1993, 63). In the 60 years following the appearance of this first translation, at least 3 other translators rendered the Grimms' story collection into English. One is *Household Stories*, an anonymous translation from 1852 to 1853. The second is *The Grimm's Fairy Tales*, by Susannah Mary Paull, writing under the name Mrs H.B. Paull. The third is *Grimm's Household Tales*, translated in 1884 by Margaret Hunt (Alderson 1993, 69).

Paull's translation has proved to be one of the most popular and enduring of any of the Grimm translations into English, being regularly republished for more than a century after its original publication (Chapelle and Williams 2007, 135; Alderson 1993, 69). However, this popularity implies nothing about the stand that Paull took in her translation. Paull's approach is one that overtly links the collection with its sources, and source authors, both in its title, and in the preface, which expresses the hope that the Grimm translations will prove acceptable to households, as their title implies (Chapelle and Williams 2007, 137). At the same time, Paull also explicitly assures readers that she has omitted only "a very few" of the tales deemed "not exactly suited to young English readers" (ibid.). These various devices clearly function to highlight the nature of the texts as translations, to emphasize the presence and importance of the source texts in the production of the translation, and to express the intention that the translations should be taken as representative of the Grimms' work, as opposed to the work of the translator or the English storytelling tradition in general. They strongly complement the overall *defensive* stand of Paull's translation.

This emphasis Paull places on underscoring the text's status as a definitive or near comprehensive translation contrasts strongly with the details of her translation practice and its resistance towards the admittance of any cultural aspects that could have been perceived as alien to her target culture (Alderson 1993, 69). Indeed, her tendency to adjust the tales has subsequently led Paull's translations to be variously described as taking "unwarrantable liberties" or being "inaccurate and stilted", or even being "a blatant distortion of the Grimms' own narrative" (quoted in Chapelle and Williams 2007, 135). Perhaps one of the reasons for these criticisms is that the number of tales that Paull's translation omits is, in fact, at least 83 (Chapelle and Williams 2007, 137).

However, omission is only a part of the strategy Paull employs in the translation of the work. Indeed, when close comparative analysis is conducted on Paull's translation and her sources, omission-based strategies are in evidence to almost the same extent as addition-based ones. Paull's approach is one that appears entirely consumed with the respective tales' potential to impart ethical or moralistic lessons on their readers (Blamires 2009, 168–169). Thus, her translations are characterized by a tendency to underscore the morality of the tale in explicit terms that are not to be found in the source text. Chapelle and Williams (2007, 139) compare Paull's translation of the *Snow White* story in her *Grimm's Fairy Tales*, with the version by Dinah Murlock in her *Fairy Book* (1863).

They find that while the "rude moral" of the text is conveyed in Murlock's translation in much the same implicit manner as in the source text, in Paull's hands the whole text becomes explicitly moralistic. Moreover, while Murlock's translation, at 2955 words, is only 136 words longer than its source, Paull's translation is nearly a third longer, at 3714 words (Chapelle and Williams 2007, 139). A majority of the additions to Paull's translation serve to underscore and explicitate the main moral message of the story, or to draw out its secondary morals. In particular, Chapelle and Williams (ibid., 139–140) point out that the endings of the two translations vary in Murlock's retaining of the torturous punishment the Grimms assign to the wicked queen, who is forced to dance at Snow White's wedding in iron shoes, heated red hot. Paull, on the other hand, has the queen's own shoes merely feel red hot as a self-inflicted result of her "envy and jealousy".

Thus, as features Paull esteemed culturally alien and unsuitable to the English target audience, the often horrific punishments doled out to the villains in the Grimms' stories were generally diluted substantially in her translations. Conversely, the implicit morals of the various stories were explicitated and exaggerated in order to conform to Paull's interpretation of the English literary system as it related to children's literature. These acts, combined with the efforts Paull makes to illustrate and underscore the nature of her text as a translation that is representative of the source text, align her translation with the *defensive stand*.

This stand was inherited by Suga Ryōhō, when he used Paull's text as the source of one of the first translations of the Grimms' stories into Japanese. He appears to have embraced Paull's tendency to downplay the punitive tone of the Grimms' stories and to cast them instead in explicitly moral terms (Noguchi 1994, 128–129). Suga's text appeared at a time when the functions of foreign children's literature in Japan were shifting away from the instruction of adults about foreign cultures, towards the entertainment and education of children themselves (Wakabayashi 2008, 233). He translated 11 of the Grimms' stories into Japanese under the pen name Tōnan Koji [桐南居士], and even though he explicitly identifies these texts as being from the "West" [西洋] in the title of the book, he does not mention that they are translations, and omits any other direct indication of their foreign origins (Wakabayashi 2008, 238). He even shifts the ideological foundation on which his translations' explicitly moralistic tone is based, away from the Christian tradition of Paull's translation, towards traditional Japanese Confucianism (Noguchi 2005, 474–475).

In Japan, freedom of worship and proselytization had been granted to Christianity, in the face of substantial resistance, around only a decade before this translation was published (Burkman 2000, 207). For more than two centuries prior to the early 1870s, Christian practice and preaching had been punishable by death (Botsman 2005, 130–131). It may be that such a short time after the religion had been controversially legalized in Japan, allowing Christianity to permeate Suga's translation would not only have identified the stories as fundamentally foreign, but may also have held the potential to alienate readers sceptical of Christianity's appropriateness for their children. Similarly, it may have been assumed at the time that the number of Japanese children with a detailed knowledge of Christianity would still be very small. Therefore, Suga's replacement of Christianity with Confucianism can be seen not only as a part of his strategy to remove explicitly foreign elements, but also his intention to facilitate the comprehension, and so education of his young readership. It was widely held in Japan at the time that including character and object names that were unfamiliar to most children would distract them from the pedagogical and didactic purposes of the stories (Nakamura 2001, 106). Thus, Suga translates Cinderella's name as お煤 [Osusu] by adding the o-prefix, common to many female Japanese names of the period, to susu (soot; Nakamura 2001, 106). Moreover, the titles of the various stories themselves rarely bear anything more than a tangential association with their Japanese translations. For example, the story known in the Grimms' German as *Die Bienenkönigin* and in Paull's English as *The Queen Bee* appears in Suga's Japanese under the title 三公子仙窟を探くる [Three Noblemen Find an Enchanted Cave].

Stylistically, however, the lexis and phraseology of Suga's translation demonstrate that his approach was far from straightforward conservatism, consumed with aligning the text with target norms. Beginning in around 1875, largely in response to the influx of translations that Japan was experiencing at the time, the traditional reliance on a written language based on archaic verb forms and phraseology that had dominated the language for centuries was challenged in the Genbun'itchi movement (Tomasi 1999, 341). This movement advocated the use of a form of written Japanese that was broadly representative of the spoken language as it was used at the time. The movement rapidly acquired a large following, and ultimately formed the basis of contemporary written Japanese (ibid., 333).

However, during the period when Suga was producing his translation, this movement was very much in its infancy. Therefore, his choice to translate using a colloquial style, rather than the classical style that still pervaded, illustrates that Suga's strategy was, in its own way, resistant to mainstream target norms of text production (Wakabayashi 2008, 239–240). It should not be inferred from this finding, however, that Suga's translation in any way mimicked the diction or writing style of his sources.

The underlying structure of the stories, which he chose to retain, on the other hand, does constitute a substantial and direct importation of foreign elements. For example, there is a structural distinction between the Grimms' stories and their native Japanese counterparts. Kawai (1995, 11) observes that the focus and purpose of the Grimms' stories is the moral core, which sees a character faced with a number of trials that are ultimately overcome, and the character's ideal marriage is the frequent reward. Japanese stories, on the other hand, rarely conclude with a wedding, but tend instead towards some state of aesthetic completeness and perfection (ibid., 120). Thus, Suga's tendency to retain the moralistic tone of the stories in his translations, albeit not in their original guise, together with their structural proclivity towards nuptial idealism, constitutes a substantial foreign feature of the texts that he retains throughout.

Suga's translation strategy, with its lack of acknowledgement of its own status as a translation, combined with its inexplicit retention of stylistic and formal characteristics particular to the source context but not the target, can be equated most closely with a *trans-discursive stand*. However, when the elements of Suga's stand are concatenated with the *defensive stand* of Paull, they produce a translation that ostensibly appears to have a very strongly *imperialist stand*. Whether or not Suga's strategy and the ultimate stand of his translation would have been different were his source text not also a translation is a matter for conjecture. However, this example demonstrates the overly simplistic nature of labelling an indirect translation purely in terms of its relationship to the ultimate source text, without taking into consideration the layers of practices bringing about such texts.

Case 3: Persian-German-English

Naturally, it is also not always the case that the first translator's stand is *defensive*, and the second's *trans-discursive*. In either case, however, the stand of the final translation does appear to tend decisively towards *imperialism*. An example can be found in the translations of the Divān [دیوان] by pre-eminent fourteenth-century Persian poet Khwāja Shams-ud-Dīn Muhammad Hāfez-e Shīrāzī [خواجه شمسالدین محمد حافظ شیرازی] into English by Ralph Waldo Emerson, via the German translation of Austrian Orientalist, Joseph Freiherr von Hammer-Purgstall.

Hāfez's work, like much Persian literature, was all but unknown to Europeans until the eighteenth century, when its translation was undertaken by a small number of Orientalists (Daftary 2006, 77). Perhaps the most widely known treatment of Persian literature during this period is that of Goethe (1819), who intimated his philosophy of translation in the "Noten und Abhandlungen" (Notes and Essays) section of his *West-östlicher Divan*. This work was inspired by that of von Hammer, Goethe's contemporary, who had already made significant inroads into German translations of Persian literature (Wahr 1941, 62). Von Hammer was moved to undertake the translation of the *Divān* into

German after arriving in Constantinople in 1799 to take up his post as translator at the Austrian embassy, and happening to hear a recitation of the text by a Persian Dervish (Shamel 2010, 22). Von Hammer goes to some effort to illustrate his conceptualization of this translation as an enriching act for the German language, and his perception of the Persian literary system as something that is not intrinsically alien to it: "Allein da die deutsche Sprache von der Griechinn und Römerinn so manches Geschmeide sich glücklich angeeignet hat, so dürften ihr ein Paar von der Schwester der Perserinn abgeborgte Ohrgehänge um so weniger fremd zu Gesichte stehen" (But the German language has so happily appropriated so many jewels from the Greeks and Romans, so a pair of earrings borrowed from their sisters, the Persians, is not so foreign to her face; quoted in Shamel 2010, 23).[1]

This explicit illustration of his conception of translation partly demonstrates the *trans-discursive stand* von Hammer adopts in his text. He actively downplays the foreign nature of the text he translates by asserting the commonality of Persians and Germans, as well as the established tradition in the German literary system of borrowing from ancient civilizations. He exhibits his relationship with the other aspect of the *trans-discursive stand* elsewhere, when he intimates that his intention in translating was to suffuse his work with the elements that define the Persian ghazal [غزل], the poetic form characterizing the *Divan*: "Wo es möglich war, Vers für Vers wieder zu geben, geschah es, und nie ist die Freyheit weiter ausgedehnt, als auf die Verwandlung eines Distichons in vier Zeilen" (Where it was possible to give a verse-by-verse rendering, this is what happened, and liberties taken with the text never extended beyond the transformation of a couplet into four lines; quoted in Shamel 2010, 23).[2]

This seemingly minor shift of expanding a couplet into a four-line stanza is, in fact, a fundamental departure from the Persian ghazal form, which pivots on its use of self-contained couplets (Kane 2009, 124). These couplets are not linked through enjambment, but instead by the fact that they all close with the same word or words, known as the radif [ردیف] (Shamel 2010, 37). A linked feature that characterizes the form in general, and the work of Hāfez in particular, is the use of indirect allusion, through the use of established metaphors, religious references, intertextuality and paronomasia (ibid., 29). The abundance and complexity of such features in Hāfez's work have led later translators to remark on the inherently unsatisfactory nature of any translation, incapable of reproducing a comparable number of esoteric, interpretive levels (e.g. Davis 2004).

The reasons for von Hammer's occasional expansion of a couplet may lie partly in German grammar. However, elsewhere, he consistently observes the formal features of the ghazal (Shamel 2010, 32). This feature, together with the fact that von Hammer does not apply a regular a-b-a-b rhyme scheme to the translation, as would have been the norm amongst contemporaneous translators (ibid., 29), illustrates the fact that he was willing to allow source norms to supersede those of the target culture. He does so, not with the apparent intention of raising his own visibility as a translator, but in order to allow the Persian literary system he perceived as superior to enrich the German system structurally as well as thematically. Lexically too, von Hammer's translation contains a large number of complex, ultimately Persian or Persian-inspired metaphors, many of which, it can be assumed, would not necessarily have been comprehensible to a sizeable proportion of his target readership. A ready example is his use of the "Tulpe" (tulip) to allude to solitude (Shamel 2010, 33).

Thus, von Hammer produced a translation that was, at the time, replete with features that would have been thematically and structurally novel to the German literary system, including manifold elements and references whose main appeal for many European readers may well have been their unfamiliarity. Simultaneously, however, von Hammer consciously and actively reduces any sense that the poetry or the source culture was fundamentally or intrinsically alien to the German literary system. His translation is, therefore, an example of the *trans-discursive stand*.

This stand was inherited by the American transcendentalist Ralph Waldo Emerson, when he began rendering a number of the ghazals into his own English translations in the years after 1846 (Kane 2009, 113). However, Emerson's own translation stand was fundamentally opposed to von Hammer's, and appears to have replaced von Hammer's estimation of the poems' enriching capacity with a focus on the poet's exotic, eastern identity (Wahr 1941, 62). Emerson's translations of Hāfez's work are significant, consisting of around 700 lines of poetry, translated throughout the last 30 years of his life (Yohannan 1943a, 407; Kane 2009, 111–112). However, Emerson's translations are also highly fragmentary, in the sense that they can be found scattered across a number of volumes, and also in the sense that many of the translated poems are far from complete, occasionally constituting only a few lines (Yohannan 1943a, 408).

Further evidence of the stand he took towards their translation appears in the fact that Emerson rarely acknowledges the sources of his translations (Yohannan 1943a, 407). In some places, he fuses two odes with similar themes (ibid., 411). Elsewhere, he produces translations that diverge to such a high degree in their content and form from their sources that identifying the precise source poem has proven problematic (ibid., 413). In some cases it has been argued that Emerson's aim was to imitate Hāfez, and that the poems should be most properly described as texts "inspired by Hāfez" or that "invoke" him, rather than as "translations" of his work (Yohannan 1943b, 26; Kane 2009, 114). For example, in one case, Emerson translates 4 German couplets into a translation consisting of 24 lines, in 6 stanzas (Yohannan 1943a, 413). Emerson was clearly more focussed on engaging with canonical Persian literature per se than on producing translations that were in any sense representative of Hāfez. Concurrently, however, Emerson emphasizes his links with Hāfez, though these were at most tangential and frequently sporadic.

Structurally too, Emerson's translation strategy differed markedly from von Hammer's emphasis of Persian literary features at the expense of German norms. Emerson's standard practice is to translate the ghazal verse form not with the radif but with a regular rhyme scheme (Yohannan 1943a, 409). In doing so, he also frequently imitates von Hammer's German word order, producing poetic translations that are neither linguistically nor stylistically idiomatic (Yohannan 1943b, 35). Thus, Emerson appears to have intended to lend his translations an air of the exotic. He was willing to copy von Hammer's word order, arguably to the detriment of his translations' lexical valence. However, he resisted von Hammer's attempts to import Persian stylistic elements, applying instead a regular rhyme scheme. These practices indicate that while Emerson was happy for his texts to be identified as foreign, he was less willing to allow them to retain features genuinely derived from the foreign source culture. Emerson's strategy, then, appears to be a clear example of a *defensive stand*. The ultimate stand of his texts, however, is a concatenation of this *defensive stand* with von Hammer's *trans-discursive stand*. Von Hammer's de-emphasis of the Persian literary system's foreign nature is not fully contradicted by

Emerson's emphasis of the same through his imitation of von Hammer's word order. Conversely, Emerson's resistance of the Persian poetic idiom, which von Hammer had actively included, reduces the texts' ability to retain genuine Persian features. Thus, since genuine features of the source culture are omitted, together with direct indications of this source culture's identity, an *imperialist stand* is the ultimate effect.

Conclusions

This article has aimed to illustrate the concatenation effect that occurs when the various stands of translators involved in producing indirect translations combine. This effect is the factor that makes indirect translations tend towards an *imperialist stand* or, more frequently, what should perhaps be referred to as a *pseudo-imperialist stand*, since any combination of *trans-discursive* and *defensive stands* will result in both omitting cultural peculiarities and reducing references to the alterity of the source text. Thus, the ultimate effect will be *imperialist* if either of the translators' stands is *imperialist*, or tantamount to *imperialist* if their stands include *trans-discursive* and *defensive* stands in any combination. Conversely, the ultimate effect will be *defective* only in the event that both translators adopt a *defective stand*. Thus, if there were an exactly even probability of each translator adopting each of the given stands, the likelihood of the second translation exhibiting a *defective stand* would amount to only 1 in 16. Conversely, because of the concatenating effect of the other stands, the probability of a second translation exhibiting an *imperialist stand* would be as much as nine times greater.

The examples employed in this article have further demonstrated that each of the stands illustrated by Robyns, and drawn on here, is not a closed set but rather a fuzzy set, and any given example can be demonstrated to be more or less closely comparable to each stand, based on the degree to which it conforms to the two identifying parameters. In particular, the examples of Feijó's and Suga's texts demonstrate that while indirect translations can take similar paths in terms of the various stands adopted by translators at each stage, the precise manifestations of these stands vary to a very significant degree, partly as a result of what is described explicitly either within the translations themselves or within accompanying material. Further research will be required to define methods for acknowledging the fuzzy nature of these sets in increasingly complex cases, while also making the conclusions built on them meaningful.

This article represents merely the first step in establishing the concatenation effect hypothesis. It remains to be seen what its conceptual or methodological boundaries are in terms of text type, genre and cultural context. It also remains to be seen whether or not there is a correlation between the degree to which individual translators are comparable with the various points on the discursive identity spectrum, and the degree to which indirect translations' stands can be compared with the *imperialist*. Future studies will also be required to establish the role of language power and prestige in influencing the stands of translators at each stage, together with the relative likelihood that a more or less hegemonic language will act as the medium of a first translation. Moreover, as already pointed out, further research will be required to discover whether second translators can actively counter the stands of first translators, and hence nullify the concatenation effect, by using secondary literature and materials to replace elements omitted, or references reduced in first translations.

Notes

1. My translation.
2. My translation.

Acknowledgements

I would like to thank Motoko Akashi for reading and commenting on the manuscript.

Disclosure statement

No potential conflict of interest was reported by the author.

ORCID

James Hadley ⓘ http://orcid.org/0000-0003-1950-2679

References

Alderson, Brian. 1993. "The Spoken and the Read: *German Popular Stories* and English Popular Diction." In *The Reception of Grimms' Fairy Tales: Responses, Reactions, Revisions*, edited by Donald Haase, 59–77. Detroit: Wayne State University Press.

Blamires, David. 2009. *Telling Tales: The Impact of Germany on English Children's Books 1780–1918*. Cambridge: Open Books Pub.

Botsman, Dani. 2005. *Punishment and Power in the Making of Modern Japan*. Princeton: Princeton University Press.

Burkman, Thomas W. 2000. "The Urakami Incidents and the Struggle for Religious Toleration." In *Japan's Hidden Christians, 1549–1999*, edited by Stephen R. Turnbull, 143–216. Surrey; Tokyo: Curzon; Japan Library: Synapse.

Chapelle, Niamh, and Jenny Williams. 2007. "Little Snowdrop and the Magic Mirror: Two Approaches to Creating a 'Suitable' Translation in 19th-Century England." In *Voices in Translation: Bridging Cultural Divides*, edited by Gunilla M. Anderman, 134–147. Clevedon: Buffalo: Multilingual Matters.

Daftary, Farhad. 2006. "The 'Order of the Assassins:' J. von Hammer and the Orientalist Misrepresentations of the Nizari Ismailis (Review Article)." *Iranian Studies* 39 (1): 71–82.

Davis, Dick. 2004. "On Not Translating Hafez." *New England Review* 25 (1): 310–318. doi:10.2307/40244407.

Goethe, Johann Wolfgang von. 1819. *West-östlicher Divan*. Stuttgard: Cotta.

Hamao, Fusako. 1995. "The Sources of the Texts in Mahler's 'Lied von der Erde'." *19th-Century Music* 19 (1): 83–95. doi:10.2307/746721.

Kane, Paul. 2009. "Emerson and Hafiz: The Figure of the Religious Poet." *Religion & Literature* 41 (1): 111–139. doi:10.2307/25676860.

Kawai, Hayao. 1995. *Dreams, Myths and Fairy Tales in Japan*. Einsiedeln: Daimon-Verlag.

Kyritsi, Maria-venetia. 2004. "The Untranslated Grimms." *New Review of Children's Literature and Librarianship* 10 (1): 27–40. doi:10.1080/1361454042000294087.

Martins, Cândido Oliveira. 2011. "Imagens de um poeta e cônsul diplomático: o Brasil visto por António Feijó." *Limite: Revista de Estudios Portugueses y de la Lusofonía* [Limit: Journal of Portuguese Studies and of Lusophonia] 5: 115–132.

Morgan, David T. 2006. *The New Brothers Grimm and their Left Behind Fairy Tales.* Macon, GA: Mercer University Press.

Nakamura, Momoko. 2001. "Power Relations in Fairy-tale Discourse: Invisible Power in a Japanese Cinderella." *Science and the Humanities* 31: 103–138.

Noguchi, Yoshiko. 1994. グリムのメルヒェン: その夢と現実 [The Grimm's Tales: Dreams and Reality]. Tokyo: Keisō Shobō.

Noguchi, Yoshiko. 2005. "英訳本から重訳された日本のグリム童話." In 児童文学翻訳作品総覧 [A Survey of Works of Translated Children's Literature], edited by Michiaki Kawato and Takanori Sakakibara, 465–485. Tokyo: Ōzorasha.

Pinto, Marta Pacheco. 2013. "*Cancioneiro Chinez*: The First Portuguese Anthology of Classical Chinese Poetry." In *Translation in Anthologies and Collections (19th and 20th Centuries)*, edited by Teresa Seruya, Lieven d Hulst, Alexandra Assis Rosa, and Maria Lin Moniz, 57–74. Amsterdam: John Benjamins Publishing.

Robyns, Clem. 1994. "Translation and Discursive Identity." *Poetics Today* 15 (3): 405–428.

Schacker, Jennifer. 2003. *National Dreams: The Remaking of Fairy Tales in Nineteenth-Century England.* Philadelphia: University of Pennsylvania Press.

Shamel, Shafiq. 2010. "Persian Ear Rings and 'Fragments of a Vessel': Transformation and Fidelity in Hammer-Purgstall's Translation of Two Ghazals by Hafiz." *Monatshefte* 102 (1): 22–37.

Tomasi, Massimiliano. 1999. "Quest for a New Written Language: Western Rhetoric and the Genbun Itchi Movement." *Monumenta Nipponica* 54 (3): 333–360.

Wahr, Fred B. 1941. "Emerson and the Germans." *Monatshefte für deutschen Unterricht* 33 (2): 49–63. doi:10.2307/30169745.

Wakabayashi, Judy. 2008. "Foreign Bones, Japanese Flesh: Translations and the Emergence of Modern Children's Literature in Japan." *Japanese Language and Literature* 42 (1): 227–255.

Yohannan, John D. 1943a. "Emerson's Translations of Persian Poetry from German Sources." *American Literature* 14 (4): 407–420. doi:10.2307/2920518.

Yohannan, John D. 1943b. "The Influence of Persian Poetry Upon Emerson's Work." *American Literature* 15 (1): 25–41. doi:10.2307/2921086.

Yoshikawa, Junko. 2010. "*Le Livre de Jade* de Judith Gautier, traduction de poèmes chinois: Le rapport avec sa création du poème en prose." フランス語フランス文学研究 [French Language and French Literature Research] 96: 15–29.

Yu, Pauline. 2007a. "Travels of a Culture: Chinese Poetry and the European Imagination." *Proceedings of the American Philosophical Society* 151 (2): 218–229. doi:10.2307/4599060.

Yu, Pauline. 2007b. "'Your Alabaster in This Porcelain': Judith Gautier's 'Le Livre de Jade'." *PMLA* 122 (2): 464–482. doi:10.2307/25501716.

Theoretical, methodological and terminological issues in researching indirect translation: A critical annotated bibliography

Hanna Pięta ⓘ

ABSTRACT

This is a critical annotated bibliography of publications on theoretical, methodological and terminological issues raised by the specific nature of research on indirect translation. It covers 19 bibliographic items (book chapters and journal articles). Each bibliographic entry is accompanied by a critical annotation summarizing the central theme of the selected publication and foregrounding its noteworthy contributions with regard to indirect translation theory, methodology and metalanguage. An introduction to the bibliography explains how the bibliographic items were located and selected. It also identifies key patterns that emerge from a brief bibliometric study of the publications collected thus far. An appendix to the bibliography contains an extensive listing of publications focused primarily on indirect translation, from which the bibliography was selected. It is hoped that both the bibliography and the appendix will provide a useful springboard for future research in the field.

Introduction

This special issue was conceived as an opportunity to foreground indirect translation (ITr), take stock of what has been done on the topic thus far, expand/challenge our current understanding of this practice, explore future research possibilities and, ultimately, contribute to overcoming the fragmentation in ITr research, launching this area of research from a scientific basis and accelerating the production of (a common core of) knowledge. This critical annotated bibliography, which gathers and comments on existing research in the field, thus serves as a useful addition to the body of research seeking to address these aims.

It should be stressed that a major difficulty in building a bibliography of publications focused on this undertheorized notion is related to the often-fuzzy conceptual boundaries that hinder a clear delimitation of its scope. Accordingly, ITr is here understood in a broad sense, as a translation of a translation. This particularly flexible and inclusive approach is more likely to reflect the complex reality of the practice, as it does not impose restrictions on, for example, the number of intervening texts or languages and therefore makes it possible to consider as ITr, inter alia, retranslation, back-translation or interlingual translations of intralingual modernizations (see Assis Rosa, Pięta and Bueno Maia in this special issue).

Before presenting the bibliographic entries, it may be useful to provide information on the sources and methods used in locating and selecting the publications included in the bibliography.

The starting point was a list of bibliographic references resulting from my prior involvement in ITr research. An analysis of these publications made it possible to obtain key items that were then used to feed bibliographic searches in translation studies (TS)-specific and multidisciplinary databases. These key items were as follows:

- 36 authors
- 42 cited publications
- 92 cited authors (including secondary, tertiary and subsidiary authors)
- 12 keywords, namely "derivative", "double", "indirect", "intermediate", "mediated", "mixed", "pivot", "relay", relayed", "second-hand" translation, "retranslation", "indirectness" (and, where possible, the corresponding terms in the other languages to which I had access, namely French, German, Italian, Polish, Portuguese and Spanish).

The bibliographic databases consulted for the purpose of this study were found in:

(a) Bibliography of Interpreting and Translation (http://dti.ua.es/en/bitra/introduction.html);
(b) Crossref (http://www.crossref.org);
(c) JSTOR (http://about.jstor.org/journals);
(d) Modern Language Association International Bibliography (http://www.mla.org/bib_scope);
(e) Scopus (http://www.elsevier.com/online-tools/scopus/content-overview#content-overview);
(f) Translation Studies Bibliography (https://benjamins.com/online/tsb/); and
(g) Thomson Reuters Web of Knowledge (http://apps.webofknowledge.com).

The choice of these databases was determined by availability at the University of Lisbon at the time when the bibliographic searches were conducted (October and November 2016). The list of references resulting from these searches was then complemented with items suggested by 14 researchers (many of whom are members of the IndirecTrans network, www.indirectrans.com) with a similar long-term interest in ITr but expertise in different languages and cultures (mainly Chinese, Czech, Dutch, French, Finnish, German, Greek, Hungarian, Icelandic, Italian, Japanese, Norwegian, Polish, Portuguese, Russian, Slovak and Spanish). The list of references resulting from these searches was saved in the reference-management software tool EndnoteX7 for selection, organization and annotation.

The selection of publications to be included in the bibliography was carried out in two stages. The aim of the first stage was to take stock of work previously done on the topic of ITr; that of the second stage was to foreground those publications that corresponded to the subtheme of this special issue (theoretical, methodological and terminological aspects in ITr research).

In the first stage, for inclusion in the bibliography the bibliographic items needed to address the topic of ITr as a *primary* issue (rather than secondary, as has usually been the case in TS) and to be *published research* (this means that unpublished MA and PhD dissertations, unpublished conference books of abstracts and unpublished conference presentations, as well as prescriptive or anecdotal writings or professional discussions, were not included). It should also be emphasized that, for the sake of consistency, publications on such subsets of ITr as retranslation, back-translation, or interlingual translations of intralingual modernizations were included only if they also paid considerable attention to other subsets of ITr. Moreover, no limits were set to publication dates other than those imposed by the existing limits of the databases consulted for the purpose of this study and those related to the accessibility of full texts. Finally, no limits in terms of linguistic/geographical scope were imposed. However, it is acknowledged that the inclusion of entries depended on my ability to make informed judgments about their relevance through my own language knowledge, from translated information available and after language consultation with qualified experts.

The list of publications thus selected is provided in the Appendix. It covers 100 works published between 1963 and 2016. While an in-depth bibliometric study is clearly needed to draw a clear picture of the emergence, evolution and most relevant features of research into ITr, a brief survey of these publications made it possible to discern the following patterns:

(a) while a small number were published prior to the year 2000 (especially in the last quarter of the twentieth century), most research in this field has appeared from that date onwards;

(b) a vast majority of studies has been confined to the translation of literature; research into indirect audiovisual translation is scant and relatively recent; research into other text types (e.g. scientific, technical) is almost non-existent;

(c) the majority of research has been historically oriented (this may partly explain why ITr is often assumed to belong to the past); research primarily concerned with theoretical, methodological and/or terminological aspects in the study of ITr has been far less frequent;

(d) the majority of publications appears to be in English (but of course the limitations of the databases consulted concerning the prevalence of research conducted in this language has to be borne in mind when interpreting this pattern);

(e) journal articles appear to prevail over other publication formats (monographs, collective volumes and chapters thereof);

(f) very few publications appear in mainstream TS or multidisciplinary journals/publishers; the vast majority is scattered among secondary journals/publishing houses;

(g) publications that feature Chinese, Iberian and Nordic languages as the ultimate source or target language (TL) appear to be most prevalent;

(h) the overwhelming majority of authors are represented by just one publication (this suggests that from the perspective of individual commitment to the topic, ITr is an incidental field of study, into which authors have brief forays, usually in the framework of their wider areas of expertise); and

(i) the overwhelming majority of publications has been authored by a single scholar (which may suggest that team efforts in the field are extremely rare).

Clearly, further research is needed to verify these patterns and to identify further trends.

In the second stage of publication selection, and in order to construct the bibliography in a manner that coincided with the topic of this special issue, an additional criterion was imposed. In particular, to be included in the bibliography the bibliographic items needed to devote at least 50% of their content (in terms of sections within a journal article or book chapter) to theoretical, methodological and/or terminological issues in the research into ITr.

A critical annotated bibliography

The 19 entries selected according to the criteria explained above are listed in alphabetical order by an author's last name and, where necessary, also chronologically (by year of publication). Each entry is accompanied by a critical annotation that summarizes the publication's central theme; foregrounds its most noteworthy theoretical, methodological and/or terminological contributions; and, where relevant, relates the publication to previous or subsequent research in the field. The discrepancy in the length of annotations was unavoidable and due to the number, novelty and complexity of particular issues raised in any given bibliographic unit.

(1) Bauer, Wolfgang. 1999. "The Role of Intermediate Languages in Translations from Chinese into German." In *De l'un au multiple. Traductions du chinois vers les langues européennes. Translations from Chinese to European Languages*, edited by Viviane Alleton and Michael Lackner, 19–32. Paris: Éditions de la Maison des Sciences de l'Homme.

This chapter, concerned with the role of mediating languages in ITrs of Chinese literature into Western languages (with special reference to German translations), makes two intriguing proposals on a theoretical level. Firstly, it suggests that in ITr chains containing three different languages, the necessary translator competence in the ultimate source language (SL) tends towards the plane of linguistic ability while that of the ultimate TL tends towards the plane of stylistic capacity. The rationale behind this claim is as follows: in this type of ITr the two features that Chinese translation theories deem as absolutely necessary in a good translation – the faithfulness ("xin") to the SL and the elegance ("ya") in using the TL – are distributed between two different (groups of) agents. Each (group of) agent(s) masters only *one* of the languages to be bridged by the translation, whilst having in common the knowledge of a third language that is neither the SL nor the TL. Second, the chapter argues that the mediating language does not have to differ from both the ultimate target text (TT) and the ultimate source text (ST) but, instead, may be a special configuration of one of these languages. There is thus a strong suggestion of conceptual overlaps between ITr and retranslation, especially if one considers – as the author does – that second or third translations into one and the same language have the benefit of a mediating language, namely the specific language of the first translator.

(2) Cardozo, Mauricio Mendonça. 2011. "Mãos de segunda mão? Tradução (in)direta e a relação em questão" [Second-hand hands? (In)direct translation and the matter of relation]. *Trabalhos em Linguística Aplicada* 50 (2): 429–441.

Drawing on examples from the contemporary book market in Brazil, this article problematizes some of the fallacies related to direct translation and ITr and reflects on their implications for the literary critique of ITr. Three points are of particular relevance in terms of the theorization of ITr. First, the article debunks the idea of an unproblematic direct relationship between the ST and TT in the case of direct translation. The rationale is that since such a translation very often involves a more or less explicit use of pre-existing texts (e.g. in the case of retranslation), this relationship is never pure, unique, unequivocal nor inaugural. Second, it draws strong parallels between direct translations and ITrs, claiming that both result from complex intertextual relationships and unavoidably perpetuate and transform these relationships. Third, the article suggests that ITrs that openly announce their indirect status should be evaluated vis-à-vis their immediate mediating texts and not their ultimate STs. This last point, however, might perhaps have been more convincingly argued by giving greater recognition to the ethical issues that such deliberate bypassing of the ultimate ST might raise.

(3) Cruz, Celso Donizete. 2007. "Sobre traduções indiretas, recepção e celebridade" [On indirect translations, reception and fame]. *Travessias* 1 (1): 1–8.

Focused on translations of literature and drawing on examples from the contemporary book market in Brazil, this article theorizes ITr from the standpoint of translation criticism. The main argument is that translation criticism could benefit from perceiving ITr as not a process but a product. The underpinning rationale appears to be that by focussing on the process one compares different elements in the translation chain and in so doing inevitably perpetuates the long-standing conviction of the primacy of the original (by tracing shifts from the ultimate ST that result from different historical iterations). However, by focusing on the product one has the opportunity to foreground differences between the corresponding texts in the target culture (e.g. various ultimate TTs to which different ITr processes from the same ultimate ST lead). It is claimed in this article that this second approach is less prejudicial to ITrs (as it avoids a priori assumptions with regard to inferiority of ITr) and could lead to the equalization of the status of ITr and direct translations, at least within the realm of translation criticism.

(4) Dollerup, Cay. 2000. "Relay and Support Translations." In *Translation in Context: Selected Contributions from the EST Congress*, edited by Andrew Chesterman, Natividad Gallardo and Yves Gambier, 17–26. Amsterdam: John Benjamins.

At the core of this chapter's argument (applicable to both written and oral translation, i.e. interpreting) is the conceptual distinction between three kinds of interlingual transfers that involve a sequence of translations into several languages: ITr, relay and support translation. The central assumption, often ignored by subsequent research, is that there are at least three languages involved in all three concepts. ITr denotes a procedure whereby a communication is established via a mediated text not intended for general consumption. The term is meant to underline the secondary importance and ephemeral nature of the mediating text, as well as the finite nature of this type of communication (since the ultimate TT cannot be reused as a mediating text). Relay, for its part, is defined as a mediation through a mediating text intended for a general audience. This definition highlights the action of the translator producing the mediating text, the multiplicity of audiences (the readership of the mediating text differs from the readership of the ultimate TT) and the dynamics in the interlingual movement of translation (the ultimate TT may well serve as a source for a subsequent translation in a potentially never-ending communication chain). The chapter further argues that there is a substantial difference between relay translation and relay interpreting: the former is claimed to lead to many more deviations than the latter. This is because in relay translation the communication chain is incomplete (the original sender recedes into the background and is typically not available to clarify ambiguities, thus weakening the fidelity to the original), whereas in relay interpreting the communication chain remains unbroken (the original sender, the mediator and receiver are all physically present and the enunciations are separated by a relatively small time-lag). In turn, support translation denotes the process in which, when translating a given ST translators consult translations into languages other than their own ultimate TL in search of satisfactory solutions to concrete problems. What differentiates support translation from relay is the degree of dependence on previous translations (in the former the translator uses isolated fragments of other TTs as parallel texts/support as part of his/her research; in the latter the entirety of another translation tends to be used a mediating text for subsequent translations). While the distinction has proven to be useful for a large body of subsequent research, it may be overly exclusive; for example, this approach makes it impossible to consider retranslations and *podstrochniki* as relayed and ITrs respectively, although it would seem reasonable that these ultimate TL-mediated translations would enter the equation if the aim were for the metalanguage to reflect real-life practices (see Assis Rosa, Pięta and Bueno Maia in this special issue).

(5) Dollerup, Cay. 2014. "Relay in Translation." In *Cross-Linguistic Interaction: Translation, Contrastive and Cognitive Studies*, edited by Diana Yankova, 21–32. Sofia: St Kliminent Ohridski University Press. Original edition, http://cay-dollerup.dk/publications.asp.

Building on examples from interpreting, subtitling and translation of literature, this book chapter revisits the distinction sketched out in bibliographic item no. 4. In so doing, it refines key definitions, disambiguates points made with regard to selected aspects of these practices and comments on the prospects for ITr and on the future of what he terms "relayed translation". The novelty of the refined definition of ITr is that it specifies that: (a) the sender, mediator and recipient know that the mediating text is merely a stage in the communication between the interested parties (thus there appears to be a close parallel with Washbourne's notion of translating for translation; see bibliographic item no. 18); and (b) there are no obvious contextual factors that affect the mediating text (since the mediator is not swayed by audience considerations). With regard to relayed translation, the following clarifications are proposed: (a) the translator producing the mediating text is not aware that this text will serve as a ST for subsequent translations; and (b) the translator producing the ultimate TT does not know what adaptations of the ultimate ST were made for the mediating text, nor does s/he have a command of the ultimate SL. All these clarifications reiterate the restrictive nature of the notions under consideration. The chapter rounds off with a suggestion that ITr research is relevant to TS in general only in the broadest terms. Recent research seems to give lie to this claim, in that it highlights the potential that exists of yielding insights useful to other fields; for example, genetic criticism (by generating new methods and knowledge about probabilistic genealogy of texts) or the historiography of intercultural relationships (by generating new data on the complex role of intermediary centres in cross-cultural transfer; see Assis Rosa, Pięta and Bueno Maia in this special issue).

(6) Frei, Charlotte. 2012. "A obra literária entre a tradução directa e a tradução indirecta ou a importância da arqueologia crítico-textual" [The literary work between direct and indirect translation or the importance of critical textual archeology]. In *Lengua, traducción, recepción: En honor de Julio César Santoyo*, edited by Juan J. Lanero Fernández and José Luis Chamosa, 195–222. León: Universidad León.

This chapter's key postulate is that one cannot study translations (be they direct or indirect) without first having established their relationship to the (ultimate) ST and, in the case of ITrs, identified the mediating texts. This claim may seem somewhat controversial given that since at least the 1970s, following the development of the target-oriented frame of reference for the study of translation, it has been considered as more than legitimate to engage in TS without the existence not only of a mediating text, but also of a ST (e.g. pseudotranslation) or a TT (non-translation). In line with the initial premise mentioned above, the article proposes a methodological framework for the identification of (various versions of) the ultimate ST and, within an ITr chain, the (various versions of the) mediating text(s). This framework is then applied to trace the genealogy of a Portuguese translation of pastoral poetry originally composed in German. On a theoretical level, the article introduces the notion of "intra-eclectic translation", defined as translation that resorts to different textual stages of the ultimate ST or the mediating text, and proposes conceptualizing the ultimate source culture as a parasite system.

(7) Gambier, Yves. 2003. "Working with Relay: An Old Story and a New Challenge." In *Speaking in Tongues: Language across Contexts and Users*, edited by Luis Pérez González, 47–66. València: Universitat de València.

This chapter examines three areas of today's society in which translating via a third language is claimed to be standard practice (interpreting, audiovisual and literary translation) and provides a brief overview of the long-standing history of ITr (e.g. Bible translation, the activity of the so-called Toledo School). To provide a theoretical background against which these two issues can be discussed, the chapter first dwells on a number of – neighbouring or currently disparate – concepts (e.g. back-translation, directionality, interlingua, internationalization, localization, retranslation, *tertium comparationis*) that are intended to showcase the ins and outs of multilingual communication. The discussion of ITr in relation to these concepts suggests that there may be correlations and overlaps between these notions, although this aspect is only briefly touched upon. Of note also is a brief concluding remark on the growing need to train translators specialized in translating for translation (i.e. those producing the mediating text and the ultimate TT).

(8) Hagerty, Miguel José. 1991. "The Rosetta Complex: Translating Translations and Theory Feedback." *Sendebar* 2: 87–90.

The first part of this article starts by exposing the fallacy of considering translation as a process dealing with only two language systems (the fallacy is said to be perpetuated by such translation theorists as Catford, Even-Zohar, Lefevere, Newmark, Nida and Steiner). It then proposes a model for describing a translator's activity that allows us to move beyond the dichotomy of SL versus TL, thus making it possible to better understand the concept of "translation of translation" (to use the author's expression). The argument underpinning this model is that the process of translation necessarily involves the extended use of all languages to which the translator has had access. The approach is named "The Rosetta Complex" after the Rosetta Stone, a secular icon for the art of translation where it is unclear which inscription (Ancient Egyptian hieroglyphs, Demotic script or Greek script) is a translation and which a translation of a translation. The model is said to be applicable only to literary translation but the underlying motivations behind this restriction are not explained. The article's second part illustrates the points made in the first with examples from various literary systems.

(9) Linder, Daniel. 2014. "Reusing Existing Translations: Mediated Chandler Novels in French and Spanish." *JoSTrans – Journal of Specialized Translation* 22: 57–77.

The article presents a descriptive exploratory case-study of French and Spanish translations of American detective novels. This case study is used as a convenient entry point for the theorization of various ways in which existing translations can be recycled across two TLs or within the same TL. Special attention is paid to the manner in which ITr correlates with concepts such as retranslation, revision, re-edition, reprint or plagiarism, etc. Particularly noteworthy is the proposal of a (partial) classification of IT, which comprises such subtypes as intralingual vs. interlingual or restorative ITr (which lessens the distance from the ultimate ST by restoring textual segments that were censored, condensed or expurgated in the mediating text) vs. its (regrettably unnamed) counterpart (which increases the distance from the ultimate ST). Equally relevant is the analytical distinction drawn between retranslation and ITr, based on the premise that the former significantly breaks or ignores the relationship chain with preceding TT(s) in the same language whereas the latter maintains this relationship.

(10) Pięta, Hanna. 2014. "What Do (We Think) We Know about Indirectness in Literary Translation? A Tentative Review of the State-of-the-Art and Possible Research Avenues." In *Traducció indirecta en la literature catalana*, edited by Ivan Garcia Sala, Diana Sanz Roig, and Bożena Zaboklicka, 15–34. Lleida: Punctum.

Focusing mainly on the translation of literature, this book chapter aims to identify the main terminological, methodological and conceptual challenges and opportunities posed by the specific nature of research on ITr. As regards terminological aspects, it acknowledges the lack of consensus concerning the metalanguage in English, adding that this has been allied with a somewhat paradoxical shortage of explicit explanations for particular terminological choices and, at the same time, contrasts with a rather undeveloped terminology in most of the remaining languages. In the matter of methodology, the chapter points to the lack of explicit models for identifying (different types of) ITr, let alone the most plausible mediating language(s) and/or text(s). On a conceptual level, it emphasizes the conspicuous lack of a consistent typology of ITr and the shortage of systematic knowledge as to how ITr correlates with other translation types (adaptation; back-translation; interlingual, intralingual and intersemiotic translation; non-translation; pseudo-translation, retranslation; revision; self-translation) or concepts such as translation norms, policy, universals and units. The chapter also stresses that it is unclear where exactly (or indeed whether) ITr begins and ends, as there are fundamental discrepancies between some of the most frequently used definitions. In an attempt to systematize the conceptual approaches to ITr, a four-level categorization of surveyed definitions is proposed, namely according to the number of languages involved (at least two languages versus at least three languages), type of mediating languages (resorting to a mediating-language version or a TL version) and intended receiver of the mediating text (TT-translator only versus wider audience).

(11) Ringmar, Martin. 2007. Roundabout Routes: Some Remarks on Indirect Translations. In *Selected Papers of the CETRA Research Seminar in Translation Studies 2006*, edited by Francis Mus, 1–17. Leuven: CETRA.

Analysing examples taken mainly from Finnish–Icelandic literary exchanges, this chapter offers thought-provoking terminological, methodological and theoretical insights, which have been very frequently revisited/re-utilized in subsequent research in the field. As regards terminology, drawing on a survey of hits returned from bibliographic searches in Translation Studies Bibliography (https://benjamins.com/online/tsb/), it usefully, though tentatively, suggests that "indirect translation" has gained ground against other competing denominations in English (without, however, specifying the type of English considered, e.g. as a native language or lingua franca). As regards methodology, the chapter is novel in that it does not shy away from offering guidelines for distinguishing direct translation from ITr and for identifying the most probable mediating language (s)/text(s). The most noteworthy contribution with regard to theoretical issues is the formulation of (more or less explicit) hypotheses concerning causes and effects of ITr. Among those that have already been tested by subsequent research are:

(a) ITr is expected to occur when acceptability is the dominant translational norm in (a part of) the target culture;

(b) ITr tends to be hidden when adequacy is the norm;

(c) ITr coincides with a low book-per-translator ratio;

(d) a translator (un)consciously takes more liberties with the mediating text than s/he would with the ultimate ST; and

(e) the grammatical structure of the mediating language(s) obscures distinctions made in the ultimate ST and (potentially) in the ultimate TT.

(12) Ringmar, Martin. 2015. "Figuring out the Local within the Global: (Sub)systems and Indirect Translation." In *Translation in Iberian-Slavonic Cultural Exchanges and Beyond*, edited by Teresa Seruya and Hanna Pięta, special issue, *IberoSlavica*: 153–178.

This article builds on examples taken mostly from inter-Nordic literary transfers. One of its main aims is to highlight the intimate connection between ITr and (global and local) hierarchies within the world system of translation. It thus pays considerable attention to the distinction between secondary and tertiary translation (also known as second-hand and third-hand translation) and to the systemic significance of this distinction. In fact, it may well be the only publication particularly concerned with the theoretical and methodological implications of distinguishing between these two types of ITr. Four points are especially worth mentioning in this respect:

(a) on the rare occasions when bibliographies acknowledge the indirect status of a translation, it is taken for granted that the translation is secondary; that is, the possibility of a tertiary translation is seldom taken into account;
(b) tertiary translation is also said to be often discarded in various mainstream definitions of ITr, as these usually presuppose the involvement of only three languages/texts;
(c) based on the collected data on Dutch–Swedish and Dutch–Afrikaans translations, the article hypothesizes on a co-relation between domestic minority status of an ultimate SL and its ITr abroad; and
(d) it is proposed that, within regional translation subsystems (e.g. Nordic), peripheral languages (e.g. Icelandic and Finnish) are much more likely to be subject to tertiary translation.

(13) Schultze, Brigitte. 2014. "Historical and Systematical Aspects of Indirect Translation in the de Gruyter Handbuch Übersetzung – HSK 26 0.1–3: Insight and Impulse to Further Research." *De Gruyter* 59 (4): 507–518.

This article reports on the results of a survey of selected entries in one of the key multilingual encyclopaedias in TS. It may well be the only contribution thus far to dedicate a substantial part of its attention to the metalanguage in ITr research. It does so with respect to English, French and German (the three languages of the aforementioned encyclopaedia), though on a necessarily limited scale (covering 35 articles touching on the topic of indirectness). One noteworthy output is the identification of the frequency with which selected designations are used: (a) in English entries the largely prevalent term is said to be "intermediate translation", with "intermediary", "indirect", "mediating", "secondary" and "second-hand" translation falling far behind and "relay" being used only with regard to the Chinese context; (b) in French entries "traduction indirecte" appears to have gained ground over "traduction" intermédiaire"; and (c) in German entries, the top-ranked appellations are "Zwischenübersetzung" and "Übersetzung aus zweiter Hand". The article argues in favour of terminological standardization of the field but acknowledges that language-bound terminological traditions may require a certain amount of historical information. On a conceptual level, it briefly proposes three variants of unpublished mediating text – "Interlinearübersetzung" ("interlinear translation"), "Arbeitsübersetzung" ("working translation") and "Rohübersetzung" ("rough translation") – without, however, providing de facto or explicit definitions for these categories.

(14) Špirk, Jaroslav. 2014. "Indirect Translations." In *Censorship, Indirect Translation and Non-Translation: The (Fateful) Adventures of Czech Literature in 20th-Century Portugal*, 132–144. Newcastle upon Tyne: Cambridge Scholars.

Taken from a monograph on the contextual and textual history of Portuguese translations of Czech literature in the twentieth century, this chapter lays out the theoretical
and methodological underpinnings for the study of ITrs (which, as is usually the case
in historical accounts of inter-peripheral literary transfers, occupy a substantial part of
the analysed corpus). One of the key claims on the methodological level (which runs
counter to the postulate formulated in bibliographic item no. 6) is that it is perfectly legitimate to study ITr without having identified mediating texts. In terms of conceptual
aspects, the chapter makes two very intriguing proposals for approaching ITr: (a) as a
form of self-imposed colonization, whereby the target (non-dominant) culture models
itself on the mediating (dominant) culture; and (b) as a symptom of what the author
terms "indirect reception," defined as the reception through the lens of another culture.
Regrettably the concept of indirect reception remains largely unexplored and the reader
is left wondering about other symptoms of this phenomenon.

(15) Toury, Gideon. 1988. "Translating English Literature via German and Vice Versa: A
     Symptomatic Reversal in the History of Modern Hebrew Literature." In *Die litera-
     rische Übersetzung. Stand und Perspektiven ihrer Erforschung*, edited by Harald
     Kittel, 139–157. Berlin: Erich Schmidt.

This book chapter delves into the history of ITr practice in Hebrew literature. Among
its most influential claims regarding ITr are:

(a) the theoretical postulate that translation scholars ought to approach the recurrence of
    (the product and process of) ITr in a culture not as a disease but as a configuration of
    interrelated syndromes that point to the underlying (inter- and intra-) systemic
    relationships related to this culture;
(b) the insistence that no historically oriented study of literature where ITrs are frequent
    can ignore the importance and implications of this practice (regrettably, the reason
    why this obligation applies only to historical TS is not explained and thus might
    lead the reader to assume that ITrs are relics of a bygone era);
(c) the formalization of an initial set of opening research queries that could potentially
    lead to the formulation of general laws of translational behaviour and evolution;
(d) the listing of the most common obstacles hindering the distinguishing of ITr from
    direct translation and the identification of the most probable mediating language
    (s)/texts(s). These obstacles are as follows: (i) the fact that many translations,
    especially those published in periodicals, still escape identification as non-originals;
    (ii) the uniformity of textual-linguistic make-up of translations from different
    languages; (iii) the dominance of an operational norm that makes it difficult to pin-
    point any trace of negative transfer in the ultimate TT; (iv) the existence of what the
    author terms "compilative translations" (defined as translations relying on the use of
    several mediating translations into one or several languages or of a combination of the
    ultimate ST with a mediating translation); and (v) the fact that, when faced with the
    lack of appropriate ultimate SL-ultimate TL dictionaries, translators producing direct
    translations tend to resort to dictionaries featuring mediating languages, which leads
    to the existence of indirectly-translated excerpts in otherwise directly translated ulti-
    mate TTs); and

(e) the suggestion of a very basic, two-step methodology for distinguishing ITr from direct translation and identifying the most probable mediating language(s)/texts(s); the first step consists in identifying contextual data on translators (their place of residence, education, language skills, access to publications) and the second in the textual comparison of the ultimate source, potential mediating and ultimate TTs.

(16) Toury, Gideon. 1995. "A Lesson from Indirect Translation." In *Descriptive Translation Studies and Beyond*, 129–146. Amsterdam: Benjamins.

This updated version of bibliographic item no. 15 was produced for inclusion in a monograph. While in the previous version of the text the theoretical and methodological postulates were presented as applicable only to the translation of literature, in the revised version these premises are extrapolated to translations from other texts. Moreover, on a metalinguistic level and with respect to the designation of the process, efforts were made to foreground the term ITr and not, as was the case in the previous version, intermediate translation (this is especially clear in this chapter's title but is evident throughout). Furthermore, on a conceptual level, the rewording of the definition of ITr leads to an important yet unheralded change in the postulated relation between the intervening languages. The previous formulation stressed that the mediating language differs from the ultimate TL, thus making it impossible to consider retranslation as ITr but making it possible to consider back-translation and interlingual translation of intralingual modernization as ITr. The revised definition, in turn, emphasizes that the mediating language differs from the ultimate SL, thus making it impossible to consider interlingual translation of intralingual modernization as ITr but making it possible to consider back-translation and retranslation as ITr. Also on the conceptual plane, the revised version adds complexity to the notion of compilative translation, mainly by suggesting this can consist of an alternate or simultaneous use of mediating translations.

(17) Toury, Gideon. (1995) 2012. "A Lesson from Indirect Translation." In *Descriptive Translation Studies and Beyond*, rev. ed., 161–178. Amsterdam: John Benjamins.

This book chapter arose out of the second revision of the chapter mentioned in item no. 15. From the standpoint of ITr theory, methodology and metalanguage, the changes introduced in this version appear less extensive than those introduced in bibliographic item no. 16. Two revisions are particularly worth foregrounding. First, further complexity is added to the definition of compilative translation, which now admits that the translator producing the ultimate TT can rely on more than one combination of the ultiamte ST with the mediating text. Second, the proposed set of contextual data on translators which is said to be necessary to determine the most probabilistic mediating language/text now includes data on the identity of people with whom the translator producing the ultimate TT established friendships and made acquaintance. This additional piece of required information thus points to potential benefits of analysing translators' formal (professional) and informal (personal) networks (in editorial boards of magazines and periodicals, in literary and artistic associations, in academies, etc.).

(18) Washbourne, Kelly. 2013. "Nonlinear Narratives: Paths of Indirect and Relay Translation." *Meta* 58 (3): 607. doi:10.7202/1025054ar.

This descriptive article revisits Dollerup's distinction between indirect, relay and
support translation (see bibliographic item no. 4) and provides some of the most relevant
insights into the conceptual, methodological and, to some extent, metalinguistic aspects of
ITr research. Among its most noteworthy proposals are:

(a) the coining of an umbrella designation "T2", meant to encompass all forms of relay
    translation and ITr;
(b) one of the most comprehensive (though not entirely systematic) sub-categorizations
    of relay and ITr, which factors in abridgements, adaptations, lost originals, modern-
    izations, pseudotranslations, self-translations, triangulations, transcreations and, at
    the same time, distinguishes between transitive and terminal translations as well as
    overt and covert modalities within retranslation, interlinear translation, plagiarism
    by translation and support translation;
(c) the profiling of relevant variables for future sub-categorizations of support
    translations;
(d) a vertical and a horizontal model for evaluating T2, the former consisting in the com-
    parison of various ultimate TTs to which different ITr processes from the same ulti-
    mate ST lead, the latter embracing the comparison between different elements in the
    translation chain (e.g. ultimate ST, mediating text, ultimate TT); and
(e) the outlining of intriguing lines of inquiry for future research, such as the questioning
    of the legal and ethical ramifications of T2, the T2 impact on the ultimate ST or the
    existence of mediating texts produced in such a way as to facilitate translation (in
    other words, a particular kind of writing for translation: "translating for translation").

(19) Witt, Susanna. 2013. "The Shorthand of Empire: 'Podstrochnik' Practices and the
Making of the Soviet Literature." *Ab Imperio* 3: 155–190.

This article offers an in-depth discussion of the microhistory of the Soviet practice of
ITr via unpublished interlinear cribs with crude rendering of the content of the ultimate
ST (termed *podstrochniki*). In analysing discourses produced by different agents of
translation (authors of the ultimate ST, censors, literary critics, translators producing *podstrochniki*, translators producing the ultimate TTs, readers, revisers, etc.), it pays special
attention to metaphors used primarily to criticize and rethink the shortcomings of *podstrochniki* practice, which is visualized as, inter alia, an equation with all unknowns, the
action of taking a death mask from a corpse or a game of blind man's bluff. Though in
a less explicit and systematic manner, the article also problematizes the ethical and legal
aspects of the action of translators working from the ultimate ST and those working
from interlinears.

A note on completeness and future updates

The list of publications from which the critical annotated bibliography was extracted (Appendix) does not lay any claim to completeness, although it may well cover the majority of

publications that fulfil the criteria mentioned above. Readers are kindly invited to provide feedback. Questions, remarks or suggestions for additional entries can be sent to hannapieta@campus.ul.pt. Future updates and revisions will be posted on the website of an ongoing ITr research project, at the University of Lisbon's Centre for English Studies (IndirecTrans – www.indirectrans.com).

Acknowledgements

The author gratefully acknowledges the precious help of Alexandra Assis Rosa, Brigitte Schultze, Cay Dollerup, Jaroslav Špirk, Javier Franco Aixelá, Katarzyna Górska, Laura Ivaska, Maialen Marin-Lacarta, Marta Pacheco Pinto, Martin Ringmar, Outi Poloposki, Pieter Boulogne, Rita Bueno Maia, Teresa Seruya, Yves Gambier and Zsófia Gombár. This help ranged from pinpointing typos, suggesting additional bibliographic items, sharing copies of missing publications, and providing language expertise to commenting on an earlier version of this contribution. Any errors and omissions are of course my own responsibility.

Disclosure statement

No potential conflict of interest was reported by the author.

Funding

This work was supported by the Fundação para a Ciência e a Tecnologia under [grant number SFRH/BPD/100800/2014].

ORCID

Hanna Pięta ⓘ http://orcid.org/0000-0002-5229-1941

Appendix.

List of publications from which the critical annotated bibliography was extracted (selected according to the criteria applied in the first stage of the selection process; organized alphabetically by author's surname).

Accácio, Manuela Acássia. 2010. "Tradução indireta: Uma prática de divulgação e enriquecimento cultural" [Indirect translation: Cultural dissemination and enrichment]. *TradTerm* 10: 97–117.
Bauer, Wolfgang. 1999. "The Role of Intermediate Languages in Translations from Chinese into German." In *De l'un au multiple. Traductions du chinois vers les langues européennes.*

Translations from Chinese to European Languages, edited by Viviane Alleton and Michael Lackner, 19–32. Paris: Éditions de la Maison des Sciences de l'Homme.

Bellos, David. 2005. "The Englishing of Ismail Kadare: Notes of a Retranslator." *Complete Review Quarterly*. http://www.complete-review.com/quarterly/vol6/issue2/bellos.htm.

Boulogne, Pieter. 2008. "The Early Dutch Construction of F. M. Dostoevskij: From Translational Data to Polysystemic Working Hypotheses." In *Translation and Its Others: Selected Papers of the CETRA Seminar in Translation Studies 2007*, 1–36. Leuven: CETRA.

Boulogne, Pieter. 2009. "The French Influence in the Early Dutch Reception of F. M. Dostoevsky's Brat'ja Karamazovy." *Babel* 55 (3): 264–284.

Boulogne, Pieter. 2011. "De Vertalingen" [The translations]. In *Het temmen van de Scyth: De vroege Nederlandse receptie van F. M. Dostoevskij*, 297–518. Amsterdam: Pegasus.

Boulogne, Pieter. 2015. "Europe's Conquest of the Russian Novel: The Pivotal Role of France and Germany." In *Translation in Iberian-Slavonic Cultural Exchanges and Beyond*, edited by Teresa Seruya and Hanna Pięta, special issue, *IberoSlavica*: 167–191.

Boulogne, Pieter. 2016. "Champion of the Humiliated and Insulted or Xenophobic Satirist?" In *Interconnecting Translation Studies and Imagology*, edited by Luc Van Doorslaer, Peter Flynn, and Joep Leerssen, 109–125. Amsterdam: John Benjamins.

Bräuner, Harald. 1988. *Die Suche nach dem "deutschen Fielding": Englische Vorlagen und deutsche Nachahmer in Entwurfen des Originalromans (1750–1790)* [The search for the "German Fielding"]. Stuttgart: Heinz.

Bubnášová, Eva. 2011. "Preklad z druhej ruky v slovenskej literatúre. k vymedzeniu pojmu a rozšírenosti prekladateľskej metódy" [Second-hand translation in the Slovak literature: The term specification and application of translation method]. *World Literature Studies* 3 (4): 79–90.

Cardozo, Mauricio Mendonça. 2011. "Mãos de segunda mão? Tradução (in)direta e a relação em questão" [Second-hand hands? (In)direct translation and the matter of relation]. *Trabalhos em Linguística Aplicada* 50 (2): 429–441.

Chen, Hung-Shu. 2016. "ヴェルヌから包天笑まで: 鉄世界』の重訳史 (特集 文化翻訳/翻訳文化" [A journey to another world: The relay translation of Iron World]. *跨境: 日本語文学研究* 3: 111–130.

Chen Yan. 2005. "20世紀中国文学翻訳中的"复译"、"转译" 之争" [Debate on retranslation and translation not from the original text in 20th century's literary translation in China]. 四川外语学院学报 21 (2): 100–104.

Chengzhou, He. 2001. "Chinese Translations of Henrik Ibsen." *Perspectives* 9 (3): 197–214. doi:10.1080/0907676X.2001.9961417.

Coll-Vinent, Sílvia. 1998. "The French Connection: Mediated Translation into Catalan during the Interwar Period." *Translator* 4 (2): 207–228. doi:10.1080/13556509.1998.10799020.

Coll-Vinent, Sílvia. 2013. "Ben Jonson's Volpone on the Catalan Stage: Rewriting a Classic through Double Mediation." *Translation Review* 87 (1): 46–58. doi:10.1080/07374836.2013.834699.

Cruz, Celso Donizete 2007. "Sobre traduções indiretas, recepção e celebridade" [On indirect translations, reception and fame]. *Travessias* 1 (1): 1–8.

Dimitroulia, Titika. 2010. "L'éthique de la traduction indirecte: le cas de Yannis Ritsos" [The ethics of indirect translation: The case of Yannis Ritsos]. In *Event or Incident: On the Role of Translation in the Dynamics of Cultural Exchange*, edited by Ton Naaijkens, 193–209. Bern: Peter Lang.

Dollerup, Cay. 1999. "New Tellers of Tales." In *The Grimm Tales from Pan-Germanic Narratives to Shared International Fairytales*, 253–286. Amsterdam: John Benjamins.

Dollerup, Cay. 2000. "Relay and Support Translations." In *Translation in Context: Selected Contributions from the EST Congress*, edited by Andrew Chesterman, Natividad Gallardo, and Yves Gambier, 17–26. Amsterdam: John Benjamins.

Dollerup, Cay. 2014. "Relay in Translation." In *Cross-Linguistic Interaction: Translation, Contrastive and Cognitive Studies*, edited by Diana Yankova, 21–32. Sofia: St Kliminent Ohridski University Press. Original edition: http://cay-dollerup.dk/publications.asp.

Domínguez, Mónica. 2006. "Traducción indirecta" [Indirect translation]. In *Traducción y literatura infantil: Érase una vez … Andersen*, edited by Gisela Marcelo Wirnitzer and Goretti Garcia Morales, 391–402. Las Palmas de Gran Canaria: Anroart.

Ďurišin, Dionýz. 1991. "Artistic Translation in the Interliterary Process." *TTR* 4 (1): 113. doi:10. 7202/037085ar.

Edström, Bert. 1991. "The Transmitter Language Problem in Translations from Japanese into Swedish." *Babel* 37 (1): 1–13.

Frei, Charlotte. 2012. "A obra literária entre a tradução directa e a tradução indirecta ou a importância da arqueologia crítico-textual" [The literary work between direct and indirect translation or the importance of critical textual archeology]. In *Lengua, traducción, recepción: En honor de Julio César Santoyo*, edited by Juan J. Lanero Fernández and José Luis Chamosa, 195–222. León: Universidad León.

Gambier, Yves. 1994. "La retraduction, retour et détour" [Retranslation, revival and detour]. *Meta: Journal des traducteurs* 39 (3): 413–417. doi:10.7202/002799ar.

Gambier, Yves. 2003. "Working with Relay: An Old Story and a New Challenge." In *Speaking in Tongues: Language across Contexts and Users*, edited by Luis Pérez González, 47–66. València: Universitat de València.

Gasparov, Mikhail. 2001. "Podstrochnik i mera tochnosti" [The interlinear and the measure of accuracy]. In *O russkoi poezii. Analizy. Interpretatsii. Kharakteristiki*, 363–372. Moscow: Azbuka.

Górska, Katarzyna. 2015. "Evidencias y contraintuiciones en la traducción indirecta audiovisual: El caso particular del documental 'Komeda. La banda sonora d'una vida'" [Evidence and counterintuition in audiovisual indirect translation: The particular case of a documentary "Komeda. La banda sonora d'una vida"]. *Transfer* 10 (1–2): 107–125.

Graeber, Wilhelm. 1987. "Eklektisches Übersetzen II: Georg Christian Wolfs 'Mährgen von der Tonne' zwischen Swifts englischem Original und van Effens französischer Übersetzung" [Eclectic translation II: Georg Christian Wolf's "Mährgen von der Tonne" between Swift's English original and van Effen's French translation]." In *Die literarische Übersetzung: Fallstudien zu ihrer Kulturgeschichte*, edited by Brigitte Schultze, 63–80. Berlin: Erich Schmidt.

Graeber, Wilhelm. 1991. "German Translators of English Fiction and their French Mediators." In *Interculturality and the Historical Study of Literary Translations*, edited by Harald Kittel and Armin Paul Frank, 5–16. Berlin: Erich Schmidt.

Graeber, Wilhelm. 1993. "Das Ende deutscher Romanübersetzungen aus zweiter Hand" [The end of second-hand translation of novels into German]. *Target* 5 (2): 215–228.

Graeber, Wilhelm. 2004. "Englische Übersetzer aus dem Französischen: Eine Forschungsbilanz der Übersetzungen aus zweiter Hand" [English translators from French: A summary of research on second-hand translation]. In *Die literarische Übersetzung in Deutschland. Studien zu ihrer Kulturgeschichte in der Neuzeit*, edited by Armin Paul Frank and Horst Turk, 93–107. Berlin: Erich Schmidt Verlag.

Graeber, Wilhelm, and Geneviève Roche. 1988. *Englische Literatur des 17. und 18. Jahrhunderts in französischer Übersetzung und deutscher Weiterübersetzung* [English literature of the 17th and 18th centuries in French translation and German secondary translation]. Tübingen: Niemayer.

Grigaravičiūte, Ieva, and Henrik Gottlieb. 1999. "Danish Voices, Lithuanian Voice-Over: The Mechanics of Non-Synchronous Translation." *Perspectives* 7 (1): 41–80. doi:10.1080/ 0907676X.1999.9961347.

Guerini, Andreia, and L. Jolkesky. 2010. "Pinóquio em tradução indireta para o português" [Pinocchio in indirect translation into Portuguese]. *Cadernos de Tradução* 25 (1): 251–258.

Hadyna, Dagmara. 2016. "A Relayed Translation: Looking for the Source Text of the First Polish Translation of Charlotte Brontë's Jane Eyre." *Studia Litteraria Universitatis Iagellonicae Cracoviensis* 11 (2): 73–81.

Hagerty, Miguel José. 1991. "The Rosetta Complex: Translating Translations and Theory Feedback." *Sendebar* 2: 87–90.

Heijns, Audrey. 2003. "Chinese Literature in Dutch Translation." *Perspectives* 11 (4): 247–253. doi:10.1080/0907676X.2003.9961478.

Hekkanen, Raila. 2014. "Direct Translation: Is It the Only Option? Indirect Translation of Finnish Prose Literature into English." In *True North: Literary Translation in the Nordic Countries*, edited by B. J. Epstein, 47–64. Newcastle upon Tyne: Cambridge Scholars.

Honeyman, Nobel Perdu. 2005. "From Arabic to other Languages through English." In *Less Translated Languages*, edited by Albert Branchadell and Lovell Margaret West, 67–74. Amsterdam: Benjamins.

Hyung-jin, Lee. 2008. "Survival through Indirect Translation: Pablo Neruda's 'Veinte poemas de amor y una canción desesperada into Korean'." *Journal of Language & Translation* 9 (2): 71–93.

Jianzhong, Xu. 2003. "Retranslation: Necessary or Unnecessary." *Babel* 49 (3): 193–202.

Jiménez Carra, Nieves. 2008. "La Traducción Indirecta de 'Los Últimos Días de Pompeya' de Edward Bulwer Lytton de Isaac Núñez de Arenas (1848)" [The indirect translation of "Los Últimos Días de Pompeya" de Edward Bulwer Lytton de Isaac Núñez de Arenas (1848)]. In *Diez estudios sobre la traducción en la España del siglo XIX*, edited by Juan Jesús Zaro Vera, 121–138. Granada: Atrio.

Kandiu, Sylvia. 2016. "David Bellos' Indirect Translation of Ismail Kadare's 'The File on H': A Contextual Analysis." *International Journal of Literary Linguistics* 5 (3). http://www.ijll.uni-mainz.de/index.php/ijll/article/view/79.

Kim, Min-so. 2007. "A Critical Analysis of the Double Translated Theoretical Books on the Humanity." *Journal of Interpretation & Translation Research Institute* 10 (2): 47–68.

Kittel, Harald. 1991. "Vicissitudes of Mediation: The Case of Benjamin Franklin's Autobiography." In *Interculturality and the Historical Study of Literary Translations*, edited by Harald Kittel and Armin Paul Frank, 25–35. Berlin: Erich Schmidt.

Kittel, Harald, and Armin Paul Frank. 1991. Introduction to *Interculturality and the Historical Study of Literary Translations*, edited by Harald Kittel and Armin Paul Frank, 3–4. Berlin: Erich Schmidt.

Landers, Clifford E. 2001. "Indirect Translation." In *Literary Translation: A Practical Guide*, 130–131. Clevedon: Multilingual Matters.

Lie, Raymond S. C. 2000. "Indirect Translation." In *Encyclopedia of Literary Translation into English*, edited by Olive Classe, 708–709. London: Fitzroy Dearborn.

Linder, Daniel. 2014. "Reusing Existing Translations: Mediated Chandler Novels in French and Spanish." *JoSTrans – Journal of Specialized Translation* 22: 57–77.

Maillot, Jean. 1982. "Les dangers de la traduction indirecte" [The dangers of indirect translation]. *Traduire* (Octobre): 11–13.

Marin-Lacarta, Maialen. 2008. "La traducción indirecta de la narrativa china contemporánea al castellano: ¿síndrome o enfermedad" [Indirect translation of contemporary Chinese fiction into Spanish: syndrome or disease?]. *1611: A Journal of Translation History* 2 (2). http://www.traduccionliteraria.org/1611/art/marin.htm.

Noguchi, Yoshiko. 2005. "英訳本から重訳された日本のグリム童話" [The indirect Japanese translation of the Grimm Fairy Tales via an English translation]. In 児童文学翻訳作品総覧, edited by Michiaki Kawato and Takanori Sakakibara, 465–485. Tokyo: Ōzorasha.

Park, Kyung-Eun, Keun-Hye Shin, and Ki-Sun Kim. 2015. "Research on Limitations of Indirect Literary Translation and Aspects of Cultural Vocabulary Translation." *Neohelicon* 42 (2): 603–621. doi:10.1007/s11059-015-0298-5.

Paul, Michael, and Eiichiro Sumita. 2011. "Translation Quality Indicators for Pivot-based Statistical MT." In *Proceedings of the 5th International Joint Conference on Natural Language Processing*, edited by Asian Federation of Natural Language Processing, 811–818. https://pdfs.semanticscholar.org/13a7/eb03cf32c11e791aa0bf84e3c602a12e357f.pdf.

Penas Ibáñez, Beatriz 2015. "The Role of Indirect Translation in the Ralentization of Cultural Modernization: The Intermediate Role of Hemingway's Early Spanish Translations." *Transfer* 10 (1–2): 51–74.

Pięta, Hanna. 2012. "Patterns in (In)directness: An Exploratory Case Study in the External History of Portuguese Translations of Polish Literature (1855–2010)." *Target* 24 (2): 310–337. doi:10.1075/target.24.2.05pie.

Proshina, Zoya G. 2005. "Intermediary Translation from English as a Lingua Franca." *World Englishes* 24 (4): 517–522.

Radó, György. 1975. "Indirect Translation." *Babel* 21 (2): 51–59.

Ringmar, Martin. 1998. "Att översätta översättningar" [Translating translations]. *Nordisk tidskrift* 74 (4): 343–364.

Ringmar, Martin. 2004. "Vägen via svenska. Om G. G. Hagalíns översättning av en finsk ödemarksroman." *Scripta Islandica*: 59–89.

Ringmar, Martin. 2007. "Roundabout Routes: Some Remarks on Indirect Translations." In *Selected Papers of the CETRA Research Seminar in Translation Studies 2006*, edited by Francis Mus , 1–17. Leuven: CETRA.

Ringmar, Martin. 2008. "Von indirekten zu direkten Beziehungen im finnisch–isländischen Literaturaustausch" [From indirect to direct relations in Finnish–Icelandic literary exchange]. *Trans-kom* 1 (2): 164–179.

Ringmar, Martin. 2012. "Relay Translation." In *Handbook of Translation Studies*, edited by Yves Gambier and Luc van Doorslaer, 141–144. Amsterdam: John Benjamins.

Ringmar, Martin. 2015. "Figuring out the Local within the Global: (Sub)systems and Indirect Translation." In *Translation in Iberian-Slavonic Cultural Exchanges and Beyond*, edited by Teresa Seruya and Hanna Pięta, special issue, *IberoSlavica*: 153–178.

Ringmar, Martin. n.d. "Indirekt översättning" [Indirect translation]. http://www.oversattarlexikon. se/artiklar/Indirekt_%C3%B6vers%C3%A4ttning.

Roche, Geneviève. 2001. *Les traductions-relais en Allemagne au XVIIIe Siècle* [Relay translation in Germany in the 18th century]. Paris: CNRS Éditions.

Roche, Geneviève. 1991. "The Persistence of French Mediation in Nonfiction Prose." In *Interculturality and the Historical Study of Literary Translations*, edited by Harald Kittel and Armin Paul Frank, 17–24. Berlin: Erich Schmidt.

Rodríguez Espinosa, Marcos. 2001. "Ideological Constraints and French Mediation in Hispanic Translated Texts: 1860–1930." *Trans: Revista de traductología* 5: 9–22.

Rónai, Paulo. 1987. "Traduções indirectas" [Indirect translations]. In *Escola de tradutores*, 25–29. Rio de Janeiro: Nova Fronteira.

Sala, Ivan Garcia, Diana Sanz Roig, and Bożena Zaboklicka, eds. 2014. *Traducció indirecta en la literature catalana* [Indirect translation in Catal literature]. Lleida: Punctum.

Schultze, Brigitte. 2014. "Historical and Systematical Aspects of Indirect Translation in the de Gruyter Handbuch Übersetzung – HSK 26 0.1–3: Insight and Impulse to Further Research." *De Gruyter* 59 (4): 507–518.

Shuttleworth, Mark, and Moira Cowie. 1997. "Indirect Translation." In *Dictionary of Translation Studies*. Manchester: St Jerome.

Sin-Way, Chan. 2004. "Indirect Translation." In *A Dictionary of Translation Technology*. Hong Kong: Chinese University Press.

Špirk, Jaroslav. 2014. *Censorship, Indirect Translation and Non-Translation: The (Fateful) Adventures of Czech Literature in 20th-Century Portugal*. Newcastle upon Tyne: Cambridge Scholars.

St André, James. 2003. "Retranslation as Argument: Canon Formation, Professionalization and International Rivalry in 19th Century Sinological Translation." *Cadernos de Tradução* 11 (1): 59–93.

St André, James. 2009. "Relay." In *Routledge Encyclopedia of Translation Studies*, 2nd ed., edited by Mona Baker and Gabriela Saldanha, 230–232. London: Routledge.

St André, James. 2010. "Lessons from Chinese History: Translation as a Collaborative and Multistage Process." *TTR* 23 (1): 71–94.

Stackelberg, Jürgen von. 1984. *Übersetzungen aus zweiter Hand: Rezeptionsvorgänge in der europäischen Literatur vom 14. bis zum 18. Jahrhundert* [Second-hand translations: Procedures of reception in European literature from the 14th to the 18th century]. Berlin: Walter de Gruyter.

Stackelberg, Jürgen von. 1987. "Eklektisches Übersetzen I. Erläutert am Beispiel einer italienischen Übersetzung von Salomon Geßners Idyllen" [Eclectic translation I: Illustrated by the example of the Italian translation of Idylls by Salomon Gessner]. In *Die Literarische Übersetzung. Fallstudien zu ihrer Kulturgeschichte*, edited by Brigitte Schultze, 53–62. Berlin: Erich Schmidt.

Tam, Nguyen Thanh. 2013. "ベトナムにおける日本文学の重訳: 歴史的背景と異文化要素の翻訳" [Relay translation of Japanese literature in Vietnam: Historical background and several translation problems]. 通訳翻訳研究/日本通訳翻訳学会会誌編集委員会 編 13: 79–95.

Tam, Nguyen Thanh. 2014. "異文化対照法としての重訳" [Understanding indirect/relay translation: Its merits as an intercultural comparison method]. 通訳翻訳研究/日本通訳翻訳学会会誌編集委員会 編 14: 157–169.

Toury, Gideon. 1988. "Translating English Literature via German and Vice Versa: A Symptomatic Reversal in the History of Modern Hebrew Literature." In *Die literarische Übersetzung. Stand und Perspektiven ihrer Erforschung*, edited by Harald Kittel, 139–157. Berlin: Erich Schmidt.

Toury, Gideon. 1995. "A Lesson from Indirect Translation." In *Descriptive Translation Studies and Beyond*, 129–146. Amsterdam: Benjamins.

Toury, Gideon. (1995) 2012. "A Lesson from Indirect Translation." In *Descriptive Translation Studies and Beyond*, rev. ed., 161–178. Amsterdam: John Benjamins.

Vanechkova, Galina. 1978. "Podstrochnik: posrednik mezhdu avtorom i perevodchikom" [The interlinear: An intermediate between author and translator]. *Československá rusistika* 23 (1): 10–14.

Vermeulen, Anna. 2012. "The Impact of Pivot Translation on the Quality of Subtitling." *International Journal of Translation* 23 (2): 119–134.

Wang Yougui. 2008. "中国翻译传统研究: 从转译到从原文译" [From translating through translations to translating from the original: China's approach to rendering literary works in "minor" languages (1949–1999)]. 中国翻译 29 (1): 27–32.

Washbourne, Kelly. 2013. "Nonlinear Narratives: Paths of Indirect and Relay Translation." *Meta* 58 (3): 607–625. doi:10.7202/1025054ar.

Witt, Susanna. 2013. "The Shorthand of Empire: 'Podstrochnik' Practices and the Making of the Soviet Literature." *Ab Imperio* 3: 155–190.

Yanhong, Xu. 1998. "The Routes of Translation: From Danish into Chinese: A Case Study of Cultural Dissemination." *Perspectives* 6 (1): 9–22. doi:10.1080/0907676x.1998.9961319.

Zabala, Karlos. 2013. "Ivo Andritxen Zubi bat Drinaren gainean eta zeharbidezko itzulpena" [An example of indirect translation: The Bridge on the Drina by Ivo Andric]. *Senez* 44: 123–141.

Zaborov, Petr. 1963. " 'Literatura-posrednik' v istorii russko-zapadnykh literaturnykh sviazei XVII–XIX vv" ["The mediating literature" in the history of Russian-Western literary relations]." In *Mezhdunarodnye sviazi russkoi literatury*, edited by Mikhail P. Alekseev, 64–85. Moscow: Izdatel'stvo Akademii Nauk.

Zaborov, Petr. 2011. "Die Zwischenübersetzung in der Geschichte der russischen Literatur" [Iintermediate translation in the history of Russian literature]. In *Übersetzung. Translation. Traduction. Ein internationales Handbuch zur Übersetzungforschung. An International Encyclopedia of Translation Studies. Encyclopédie internationale de la recherche sur la traduction*, edited by Harald Kittel et al., 2066–2073. Berlin: Walter de Gruyter.

Zhang Yi. 2003. "转译——种被无视了的翻译现象" [Translating from the intermediary language: An ignored translation phenomenon]. 重庆工学院学报 17 (6): 109–111.

Zilberdik, Nan Jackques. 2004. "Relay Translation in Subtitling." *Perspectives* 12 (1): 31–55.

Zubillaga Gomez, Naroa. 2015. "(In)direct Offense: A Comparison of Direct and Indirect Translations of German Offensive Language into Basque." *Perspectives* 23 (4): 1–12. doi:10.1080/0907676X.2015.1069858.

Zurbach, Christine. 1996. "Traduction indirecte et hiérarchie des littératures" [Indirect translation and the hierarchy of literatures]. In *Literatura Comparada: Os Novos Paradigmas: Actas do II Congresso da APLC*, edited by Margarida L. Losa, Isménia de Sousa and Gonçalo Vilas-Boas, 317–322. Fundação Luís Miguel Nava.

Zurbach, Christine, and Tânia Alexandra Marques Filipe e Campos. 2005. "A recepção do teatro nórdico em Portugal: O caso da tradução indirecta das peças de Strindberg" [The reception of Nordic theatre in Portugal: The case of indirect translation of plays by Strindberg]. In *Actas do colóquio internacional: Relações literárias franco-peninsulares*, edited by Ana Clara Santos, 115–126. Lisboa: Colibri.

Index